The writings in this book are bold tender; quite a combination to into her life both physically and ~~emotionally~~ ~~as~~ ~~one~~ ~~grapples~~ with what it means to be fully awake. There is a vulnerability. The line, *"I need to be wanted,"* stopped me in my tracks as I recognised it is perhaps the fundamental wanting of any human. She explores the complexity of relationships in an unflinching and provocative way, but there is that tenderness in the exploration. And through it all, Georgia's humour shines through as does her wonder towards life.

Jules Swales, M.A.

Creativity Coach and Mentor
Author of *I want a Stonehenge life* and
Declarative: 33 Statements that Changed my Life

Naked is the perfect title as Georgia lays herself bare in this honest and raw writing. Holding northing back, her beautifully descriptive and poetic language immediately transports the reader into the scene she is portraying...

Julie McCammon

Physiotherapist, Myofascial Release Therapist.
Body Mind Coach. Author of *Finding Mystery Within* and *Quiet Mind Quiet Body*

This book gets to the heart of what it means to be human. It is tender, poetic, raw, and honest. It touched places deep within my soul, made my heart ache, and had me laughing out loud.

Georgia has a rare way with words, and she uses this gift to share her lived experience as the daughter of a narcissistic mother. She expresses sorrow, strength, and the beautifully messy reality of being both human and a spiritual being. I know this book will impact many lives.

Nicola Jayne Drew

Psychotherapist, Trauma Specialist, and Soul Alignment Guide. Author of 6 books, including *From The Heart: Explorations in True Nature and Unconditional Love*

Wow! I have just raced through reading *Naked* and I am speechless and blown away. Reading it has brought me to tears with rage, shock and sadness, bringing some deep-seated memories to the fore. But reading it has also given me laughter, wry smiles and, ultimately, a further understanding of the Human Condition.

Such brutality, terror, shame, bravery, joy, pleasure, authenticity, disgust, sexual abuse, mental abuse – feelings of duty, longing and not giving a damn about what people think. But the overriding theme is LOVE in all its shapes Incredible – just incredible!

Olivia Eisinger

Editor

NAKED

HEALING THE NARCISSIST'S DAUGHTER

GEORGIA BAZIN

First published in Great Britain in 2025
by The Naked Truth.love press

© Copyright Georgia Bazin 2025

A CIP catalogue record for this book
is available at the British Library.

ISBN (Paperback) 978-1-0684372-3-6
ISBN (Hardback) 978-1-0684372-4-3
ISBN (eBook) 978-1-0684372-5-0

Dedication

The wind that lifts my wings in magnificence is my
Unit of humans and animals.
Philip, Oliver, Bianca and Tobias.
Your journey to unfurling your wings, I watch with love.
Coco, Suki — just love in motion.
And my **unexpected** teacher, Jac the Jackdaw,
The little bugger of a corvid who rules this roost,
Who shows me exactly where I am in my presence.
I love you all.
Thank you, God.

This book wrote itself before I had conscious awareness
of it being a thing. I've turned up to its evolution with each
new insight and opening of the computer each day. Life and
creative genius do that. It's been raw.

I am the dancer who cares not who is watching.

Gx

A Note About The Cover

Adam and Eve, a snake, a tree and an angel is where our human story starts. I was schooled with the Bible, though I am not religious. It's a beautiful creation.

My book cover had many varieties of faces. I had got so noisy in my head as to what was a bestselling book cover, the sort that made people go, "I must read that," and I asked so many opinions when nothing quite felt right – I forgot to get quiet and listen to myself. So it happens I had booked a solo visit to Polperro in Cornwall at the most perfect time I needed to listen. I took bags of paints and canvases that just seemed right to take. The first night I had booked a tiny shepherd's hut and went off to sleep, slept the most deepest sleep I have had for a while, woke up and I just had an image.

I pottered off to Polperro. It's so quaint and pretty. Set myself up in the kitchen in the deep window seat where the sky was my light. I'd wake up and sit starkers painting, then potter off to the beach, swim and write. Stay up late, wake up late. This small painting took me my whole 5 days away. I drove away with the oil still wet.

The story of Adam and Eve, a snake and an apple from the tree of knowledge is embedded in many cultures. Adam was made of the earth, Eve from his rib. They lived in the Garden of Eden, heaven on earth. The snake, a metaphor for the ego, mind and judgement, lured Eve into a juicy bite saying, "You need knowledge". Adam and Eve fell into their mind and for the first time knew self-consciousness, separateness, and covered their naked bodies. An angel guarded the Tree of Knowledge after. Adam and Eve were sent out into the world to become fully human with all that entails. Pain, joy, love, grief and all we experience in this human life and a forgetting of being one thing only. They searched for the remembering to come back home whilst being in a human life. To live in bliss of knowing they were a truly divine being in skin and bones.

This life will always be a co-creation of our spiritual nature and DNA with the mind thrown in for a canvas. We were born with freewill to choose the creation we live.

Content Note

This memoir includes descriptions of child abuse and trauma. Some readers may find the content distressing or triggering.

If you are affected by anything in this book, please consider reaching out to one of the following organisations for support:

Three Principles Global Community
https://3pgc.org

Samaritans
www.samaritans.org

NSPCC
www.nspcc.org.uk

Rape Crisis England & Wales
https://rapecrisis.org.uk

You are not alone…

IT'S ALL MADE UP
AND
IT'S ALL TRUE
AT THE SAME TIME.

we are each a
unique novel
waiting for edits,
and sometimes
whole re-writes.

THE SOFTWARE

I came preloaded on 8th April 1964. Then was named Georgia. Aries, Wood dragon, Number 5 if you're counting. Human designed Generator 4/6. I identify as Enneagram 9 – The Peacemaker. I am right-handed, blue-eyed, with a leaning towards fatty liver and diabetes. A predilection for shoes and dancing. I don't sleep enough. A craving for learning. I know there's a god, she isn't religion. I like pink, not so enamoured with orange. There are women I love and certain men I just know are flames. I hear the dead and angels. I like options and pens. Want to be loved in some undefined way. Always thought I don't fit in but what's "in" and who decides? I'm curious and like adventures. A healer and artist. I swim in cold water and always sunbath topless. Optional extras are not included. Life in-app purchases have been necessary.

With Love and blessings
Georgia

Coaching: www.georgiabazin.com
Book publishing: www.thenakedtruth.love
Direct email: georgia@georgiabazin.com

MY Fear IS THAT I
MISS MY Magnificence

contents

Foreword   1

Daughter to Mother   5

Prologue   7

Introduction   19

Overdressed   27
Chapter 1 - The Creation   29
Chapter 2 - The Hurt   59
Chapter 3 - Messy Stuff Living   85
Chapter 4 - The Unseen   113

Undressing   131
Chapter 5 - Loss   133
Chapter 6 - Body   181

Naked   203
Chapter 7 - Finding   205

References   277

Index for Individual Piece Titles   279

Foreword

"Be tender with me, I've come a long way, past broken bridges and empty riverbeds dust-filled, blown by vacant winds."

Georgia Bazin, *Limitation – Where Are You?*

These are tempestuous times for women. Then again – have they ever not been?

Over the course of my 71 years, I've watched women's voices, rights, and reflections lurch forward in fits and starts. Sometimes blazing at the forefront. Sometimes flickering quietly in the background. Now, again, we face a fierce backlash – by some men and even some women – seeking to return us to the places we were once told we belonged: Pigeon-holed. Costumed. Silenced.

In the late 1970s, psychologist and philosopher Alice Miller wrote *The Drama of the Gifted Child: The Search for the True Self*. By "gifted," she didn't mean academically advanced. She referred to children who survived unthinkable cruelty by numbing themselves, silencing their truth in order to endure. Some, she observed, go beyond survival. They reclaim their inherent gifts. They uncover their true story. They speak.

But how? How does survival triumph?

Fast forward to 2006. A grassroots phrase – *Me Too* – sparked a reckoning. Gaining momentum a decade later, the movement helped survivors of abuse and harassment speak out, step forward, be seen. Yet, as with Miller's work, it left us with pressing questions: What now? After the crying out, after the rage and reckoning — how do we heal?

In her book *Naked: Healing the Narcissist's Daughter*, Georgia Bazin offers profound, poetic answers. Through memoir, photography, and painting, she reveals what it means to shed the roles, masks, and identities we've been given or forced to wear. She declares — beautifully, powerfully — that we are not our stories. We are not what was done to us. We are not the names we were called or the silence we endured. We are, always, a blank canvas — divinely inspired, sovereign, creative, and whole.

When we find the courage to drop the costume of thought, we uncover a truth: *our nakedness is not shameful.* It is our essence. It always was. It always will be. No narcissistic parent, no abuser, no institution or culture or creed can ever take that away from us.

If your heart is open, prepare to be shaken. Georgia writes with unflinching vulnerability about childhood sexual abuse, parental neglect, and the slow-burning grief that accompanies such pain. You may weep. You may rage. You may want to look away.

But stay with her. Because woven into every page is a golden thread — of tenderness, empathy, forgiveness, audacity, rebellion, and love. Georgia's creative fire dances through her words as she recounts her journey through childhood, maidenhood, motherhood, and into sovereign adulthood.

Her path to reclaiming wholeness has not been linear. Few truly are. But through the mosaic of brokenness and divinity, pain and transcendence, Georgia emerges – poetic, raw, luminous. Potent.

"I hold my own hand often as I go to sleep to remind myself there is a part of me so loving... and it never left."

Georgia Bazin, *The Paradox*

That image will stay with me. Perhaps with you, too. In the simple act of holding our own hand through the drama of life, we remember we are not broken. We are a loving wholeness. A living, breathing essence that caresses us always, even when others cannot.

Linda Sandel Pettit, Ed.D.

Spiritual Strategist, Author, Intuitive Guide, Former Psychologist

Dau6HTer To MoTHer

My mum has always been an artist. She's a painter, designer, dancer and healer. So, when a few years ago she took up creative writing, it was little surprise that she took to the new outlet like a fish to water. Her dedication to the practice amazes me; she writes every day, whether in car journeys, sat in dingy waiting rooms, or huddled away for hours in her study.

When she wrote her first book, *Love, Liberation and Libido: Divinely Feminine Poems and Prose*, I was blown away by what she had created and I told her I was proud of her, which still feels like a strange thing to say to a parent. In her usual way, she shrugged it off, as many women do, but especially those who never had parental recognition. I then asked if she was proud of herself. She stuttered, as though she had never been asked this question before, "I guess so," she said.

This book has been in the making for a long time. I've seen drafts and redrafts of the manuscript, watched as this work has evolved and flourished into the book you hold into your hands today. And to say I am proud of my mum and what she was created, is the biggest understatement in the world. I am *astonished* by her creativity, her vulnerability, and her dedication to put her experience into the words on these pages to help others who have also experienced narcissistic parenting.

Reading this work has allowed me to see my mum in a new way. It's given me an understanding and insight that a child rarely sees in their parent, and it is brave to hand it over to the world. I hope that the readers gain some insight, resonance, or at least get to giggle at the photos of my mum's bras. And I hope, above all else, that my mum can see what a magnificent inspiration she is.

I love you, Mum.

Bianca Bazin

prologue

naked

I heard Rick Rubin say, "I write a book only for me," rather than the audience, in his podcast interview with Andrew Huberman (see References). I heard that somehow what I say is what someone will need to hear. In my deepest dark moments something always appeared; it could be a random comment or line I read, or heard someone speak, but there was no formula for relief, no one place to go to that I knew would let me see light and shift my level of understanding or consciousness. Sometimes the impact came from unexpected lines in a Hollywood movie, and as I heard them, I thought the script writer had in their head a deep mystical understanding of life and how I worked. They were lines that somehow slipped in to catch someone, me, who needed to hear. The one thing I realised is the words that impact me may not impact you, so I'd ask you keep reading with an open mind. There is no one prescription to either a happy or miserable life except a question "Is what I think true?" which seems to be the very last question we remember to ask ourselves. This book is about that very question — Who or what am I if I am not that story in my head? And who is everyone else?

What is the Naked reality of me and the world around me stripped back? How do I feel and see safety in a world that looks chaotic? I so wish I'd known to ask this question decades ago and to instil it in everyone I ever had a conversation with and love.

To simply question all the things, I was so sure about myself, because so much had to fall apart, die, and leave me and as a human being, I didn't like that idea, it just looked like more chaos. My mind is a control freak that looks like a terrifying option. My mind likes the illusion of "I have this" when it has nothing at all except ideas. Ideas that change nothing outside but colour my inner vision of what's outside.

"Is what I think true?" asked by eight billion people may show us the truth — **we all think**. We all think the same theme of thoughts — some just speak louder to each unique person. So simply I think, and it creates my reality, the glasses and filters I see life through.

I hope there will be a moment or a line that will make you go, "Holy Fuck, that's it!!" but I have no guarantee. All I can do is tell you how I found my G-spot as I stripped off and how I continue being naked with myself.

It hasn't been simple.

walking with angels

I came out of a deep sleep having a conversation with an angel who said to me, "Ask me for guidance and help – that's what we are here for. I always have your back. We are all celestial. You're all angels, ordinary everyday angels."

I felt the nudge to go to the sea; it was 7.35 am this morning as I walked along the beach in Tenerife and the sun rising just above the dark mountains that hug the coastline. I picked up a cup of coffee from the buffet as I headed to the dark sand and choppy water for a swim while the masses were breakfasting or sleeping off the night before. I passed a young man with dreadlocks, feet hanging over the edge of the path, smoking a spliff. I detest the smell – it's acrid and rude on my nostrils when I can smell the sea.

The sea overnight deposited messy seaweed, yellow and bobbly with seeds – a team of men scooped it up to make the beach look pristine. As I walked through the residue, there were remnants of plastic, a used condom, bits of trash, an empty bullet casing, the tattered remains of a sanitary towel floated in the water whilst small yellow crabs scuttled across the sand.

I walked into the water between two lines of buoys, the sand empty of anything under my feet, scraped clean by rough waters. I swam out and just hung in the water, letting its motion move me. I found myself out past the lines of buoys, and I had the realisation that this is what the book has

asked me to be — outside my lines and comfort zones. To talk about things that aren't talked about. It has required me to touch places I have been frightened of, but in essence, this journey of healing and understanding has always been that anyway, combined with sheer ecstasy and freedom.
I am reminded that what I clear today may be washed up tomorrow to be seen anew with different eyes. That my head demons are very clever at hiding but once I get a view of truth it might take me a while to see it — I know clarity is there to see, often with a feeling of "I can't believe I didn't see that" and a laugh or tears at the simplicity I'd missed.

As Sydney Banks said, "If we could just learn not to be frightened of our experience," what we think about it, and instead, "listen for the feeling" we would be all good.

I walked back along the black sand, the sun making diamonds of the shards. I am exactly where I am meant to be always, as is this book.

LaDLe WITH Love

I relish telling people I love them. A nourished me nourishes other people. I have more to give away, more space in a stuffed full heart. In abundance I have a heart so full of love to give and spread, like rose-petalled strawberry jam on an oven-warm scone or a toasted butter-dripping succulent slice of sour dough. I hurt sometimes, I am so full to bursting, the stitching on my seams expands and contracts I get scared and tuck myself away.

I think I broke a little in the abuse and cruelty around Mummy and then her death. A heart that desperately ached as I watched her die into coldness, a rerun performance of life. So intense the pained ache, a tight corrupt fist clenched to stop me pumping. Unnourished I starved for many decades, emotionally anorexic for acceptance by parents. I have this sharp little feeling floating around slicing paper-thin veins and bleeding out to stem. I am worthy of loving, though I misplace this sometimes, often in the knife drawer with the nicks and scabs I am bound to. Nourishing me nourishes others, it works both sides of the toaster. I find it hard to be fed, lacking the trust it isn't arsenic inside — acrimoniously poisoned in what looks like nice. Trust-less is a barren habitat, a fruitless land.

I am growing new seeds, feeding myself. My mother teacher, a hater of feminine, wrapped and cellophaned me in female malnourishment. I love in my words to the people I know, so they are resplendent in understanding and doubtless of their worth to me. I want a two-ended spoon, one for you and one for me. A balanced diet to safely ingest and absorb the nutrients of loved acceptance. I love you — in case I forget to say later, dear reader.

New Seeds.

Naked is the most vulnerable place to live. The grandest, greatest adventure. An intimacy with life and myself.

SKINNY DIP

June 2021 after Covid lockdowns I booked a week on a tiny private island called Erraid next to Iona, and tide dependent, attached to the Isle of Mull, in Scotland. A mile-square, unkempt eagle swooped, and sheep munched land that had remained uncluttered by humans, technology and speed. A row of stone-built cottages inhabited by six island keepers, a group of long-term retreaters from the buzz of life. They grew vegetables and ate vegan chocolate. No phone signal.

I got the week between rain and more rain that the sun shone. All the dwellers decided to go swimming, so I grabbed a bikini and headed off down Caribbean-like sandy beaches. We climbed and walked the quietest grassy island arriving at a beach of fine white sand enclosed in granite cliffs dusted in white daisy flowers and clinging ferns, to the clearest water. Off came everyone's clothes; I followed, hesitant. A mixture of bodies unveiled themselves and pottered down to the water. I remember thinking, what if my body simply was beautiful and what if it didn't matter what anyone thought — I would only be guessing.

I skinny dipped so many times that week whether there were boats in the bay or not. I took pictures of myself and surprised some boat travellers! They seemed to not mind and just smiled and said hello!

I changed that week. My body is precious and unique but not designed by me. My bits are the same as everyone unless they are a fella, and fella's bits are unique but similar. None of us picked them. My body is delicious for a human experience and in the quiet I knew I was what inhabited it. Naked was being vulnerable and that was safe and divine.

Introduction

Beginning

The story of me started creation before I was born. I am an energetic creature. The light that comes as an egg and sperm unite — it's called the zinc spark, when biology and spirit come together, a viable union of a being. Every thought my mother had, every thought my grandmother had, is felt when in utero. Every word has a feeling. I came with patterns and responses already known that weren't even mine. I am an energetic echo of information. I have masks that aren't mine. I have learnt information in my system not about me. I am cloned from my mother and all the generations before in my biology and chemistry. I contain a cluster of energy information that's ancient. I am a chimera. Sometimes I feel something, and I haven't got a clue what it is, my body just has a feeling and I wonder where it came from, as if it remembers something I have no conscious awareness of. My generational curse is avoidance, but pain demands to be felt and healed. Pain travels through families until someone is ready to face and feel it.

I am that someone.

I am a healer. It's time for a searching healer to understand and share her journey.

Safety and stability aren't a thing being the daughter of narcissists when you don't know you are. I lived in a shadow I was so used to that I didn't know it was there, I didn't even know I had a shadow of my own. I became a pleaser, exposed to hurt. I walked it in everyday life, life inside an unseen shroud. An expectation of pain in whatever way I encountered it.

I use the word 'mummy' as a 60-year-old woman and mum myself. My writing teacher asked me recently, didn't I think it kept me in a childhood state with my emotional relationship to her? I called her Mum but addressed cards to 'Mummy'. When didn't I feel her wrath, judgements, anger, jealousy or general unhappiness in life? I was the brunt or the dumping ground, I could be either depending on what she needed — I always provided her with the victim of her choice. I called her Mummy when I said, "Mummy, I love you" and I would hug her. I always hugged her, her often stiff and unyielding body, her armour. 'Mummy' just seems more endearing and something I've got used to since she died. It adds a softness to our harsh relationship. I used to wish I could go back and rewrite our time together with softness and love, I still do. An adult fairy tale without knowing the whole truth. What happened made me who I am today. Sometimes I hated her, often didn't like her, but underneath all that, I loved her.

Mummy, whose name was Patricia Joyce, wanted to be unquestionably unjudgementally loved, yet she was unable to do this for another person. She was obsessed with holding on, controlling her safety and money — her ecstasy drug.

It seems I've always been the opposite in the wish to not hold on and in. I learnt money was dangerous; blackmail and evaluation its purpose.

Absent fathers whose pattern of abandonment created a message in me, something deeply hurt lived within me that I didn't see until I was 60. Men seem to walk away easier; I wonder if it's because they didn't carry a child in them. I am wired different. There are societal ideas, conditioning and programming, basic instincts in my ancient brain. It's not about fighting and striving to achieve. I learnt there is a natural process that simply happens, and I am the vessel for it to come into the world. I'm really blessed to be woman, I may not be simple, I don't think about sex so often in the day. I experienced birth of a human body, I understand that process with this book, the devotion to nurturing something into the world and being frightened of Being Naked.

All parenting says something to a child – every child simply wants to be loved and safe.

I didn't feel it.

CHIMEras

Organisms, organs or parts consisting of two or more tissues of different genetic composition.

I am a body that contains the cells of each of my children, three alive and one departed. Each of my children and I have cells of my mother, grandmother, my mother's siblings that she shared with me. I share cells with the baby she birthed before me. The baby boy she had adopted contained his mother, grandmother and all her babies' cells. My children have cells of each other before them. We all are biological echoes of generations.

The cells of others have been found in a mother's bones, heart and brain. The stem cells of babies rush to heal damage in a mother's body, so beautifully designed that the child becomes the mother's healer.

We are all connected energetically and biologically in ways that we don't see, not by any bodies choosing; it's natures brilliance. Somewhere, we all came into existence from one biology, one starting place whether it was a bacterium from the ocean or Adam and Eve. We are an evolution of energy into matter. A miracle of creation, evolution and intelligence.

RE-MEMBERED –
BITS OF EXPERIENCE
STITCHED BACK
TOGETHER
CREATE FRANKENSTEIN'S
MONSTER – IT'S ALL IN
THE MOVIE!

FUCK OFF

I stood in the hospital car park beside my opened car door, the incessant bleeping warning me it was ajar with the engine idling running diesel. On the iPhone in my right hand, Barbara, Mummy's friend, asked me about her prognosis. I looked up at the window, on the other side of which I knew she lay wrapped in a flowered white and blue hospital gown. In the wrinkled crevice of her elbow, a cannula allowed the entrance of life-saving penicillin.

"Will she be okay?" Barbara said. Between breaths, I felt Mummy's searching soul surround me in last night's crumpled pink linen dress. A warm August sun reflected off silvered windows. Coldness burrowed my skin, trying to get in, own, and use me. I felt her intention; her body frail; she looked to me for her new home.

"Fuck off, you've had so much of my living," I shouted towards the window. "Your body's up there; go back to it, leave me alone. I won't be your victim anymore." To Barbara, I said, "Mum's soul is travelling"; Barbara got it, she's psychic too.

OVERDRESSED

CHAPTER 1

THE CREATION

WOMB

I hear your heartbeat   When it falters I learn terror   I
know your fears   They live me   I am your anxious sadness
in every pump of blood we share   I am nourished on your
chemistry   I cry the tears you shed   The caress of your
laughter lingers long after   We are cellular together
connected   I hear the imprint of your mother   her mother
I am cohabiting with generations of echoes I am ancient
I'm learning for my arrival in the words you speak   The
feel of you is me   I am a holder of others knowledge
Patterns and behaviours   Feelings and thoughts   You
share them all in innocence   I am a learner before being
birthed You give me a name and teach me to be separate.

canvas

I am child I love.

I am child I learn.

I am child I survive.

I am child I revolve around you.

I am child I don't know adult.

I am child I copy.

I am child imagination

I am child being created.

I am child I sense.

I am child I am your words.

I am child I don't question.

I am child I don't know.

I am child innocent.

IT'S SURVIVAL

Mummy cries — What did I do?
Mummy doesn't want to play — Doesn't she love me?
Mummy is busy — I am a nuisance
Mummy cries — What did I do?
Mummy shouts — I need to hide
Mummy tells me I'm naughty — I'm naughty
Mummy says I give her a headache — I must be quiet
Mummy is angry today — I get frightened
Mummy cuddles me — I am protected
Mummy laughs — I like to please her
Mummy is cross — I like to please her
Mummy smacks me — I panic
Mummy kisses me — I am loved

Daddy is loud — I am scared
Daddy is angry — I don't understand
Daddy shouts at Mummy — I am scared
Daddy smells funny and is rough — I'm in danger
Daddy hugs me — I love Daddy
Daddy sends me to bed — I'm cross
Daddy doesn't talk to me — He doesn't love me
Daddy ignores me — I want attention
Daddy doesn't play — Not fair, I want to please him
Daddy fills a glass with whisky — I need to be good — danger
Daddy tells me to be quiet — I'll be a mouse

Quiet   Pleaser

Conform   Hide

Invisible   Attention

Danger   Believer

Fear   Freeze

Love   Run

Protection   Defence

Peacemaker   Voiceless

Loud   Trusting

Loyal   Dreamer

peter and patricia

one word embroidered at a time

I am the biology of Patricia and Peter   Jaded through school
Teenage prevalence for trashy novels, boys and secret
fags   Unsignposted except in dance   *Dance like no one is
watching. No one was*   Sad teenage songs   Wrangler jeans
A hippy born too late   Surrendered dreams   Scrubbed
clean by parenthood   Woven into me no voice   Woven into
me no choice   Married at 19   submissive daughter
aged 52

our memories
don't tell us
how to use them

ABSENCE

Yellowed pictures of me
I've inherited,
My story of childhood,
No
Birthday cake,
Bath time games or stories read,
Playing on a beach or taking a walk,
My memory blank,
I am their absence.

I remember gooseberries in a big garden.
Their hairy bitterness,
At 4, meeting a man,
His deep gaze carving a memory,
My absent biological father,
My brother killing a kitten,
It ran around in pain, screamed until it dropped,
I remember my black eye from my un-biological father,
His drunkenness,
The cupboard I hid in,
Behind clothes in the musty wardrobe,
Eyes closed and ears plugged,

The day we drove away with the cat,
I was 6,
I remember wetting myself at ballet class in a new school,
A puddle of shame,
Joanne and me,

As fledgeling bodies
Curious about
Naked
Under her bed,
My brother and I as different planets,
A mother ruled existence,
Quiet fathers,
I was always vetted
As her understudy,
I don't remember about myself,
How I felt, what made me happy or sad,
What I liked, except Camembert triangles,
I was never unearthed.
I was a peacekeeper.

secrets are carnage

Ugly I am
Invisible I am
Unsafe I am
No one sees
Secrets under my skin.

SILENCE IS NOT
GOLDEN
A VOICE IS MY GIFT.

UGLY

I gave him head, swallowed down — I was 9 maybe 10.
Prepubescent unbudded breasts under the orange and
yellow flowers of a dress I didn't own. He didn't touch me
simply his hand on my head, cock in my mouth. He told me
suck. He sat bare-bottomed on a white commercial chest
freezer, trousers pleated around his hairy ankles. Belt coiled
snake-like at my feet. The hotel deputy manager with his
prick in a child's mouth. Ugly nourished. A cancered shadow
I carry concealed from view. I sit here empty. A ghost, quiet
five decades. Havoc swallow filthy filthy swallow swallow
fucking swallow you filthy child child you're filthy to swallow.

I am a vault locked with incomprehension. My fucked-
up antenna shows it's halfway between stations in each
encounter with a human with a phallus. I am the twisted,
dirty, ugly child who swallows everything down, with guts
that want to puke. I am gagged in the thrusting of I don't
understand. I am this secret, morbid, craven and grubby.
Naked yet clothed. Ugly grew askew, I am damaged goods.
The façade of okay. Throw the damaged goods away,
garbage for collection. I swallowed abuse and sit here
empty, tearless and mutated. Please don't be nice. I'm ugly.
I was noticed as compliant.

Biological

I need to be wanted
To matter
From a hidden place
Created by
A father that walked away
So easily
Left me a quiet child
Too young to know
It
Wasn't About Her

'Pick me, pick me,'
I've silently emitted all my
Days
Every time someone picks
Someone else
My 'pick me' voice has
Stuck on the Elastoplast
Of 'it doesn't bother me'
I'm fine with
This
Unwantedness

All the Elastoplast contained

Was my temporary anaesthesia
Until
My next 'pick me'
Moment raised her
Head
Powerless
To ask to be picked

A life lived from
A craving
To be wanted and
Cherished
Remember, when you walked away
I didn't know
it
Wasn't About Me.

PeTer THe RePeaTer

I was 18 the day she told me Peter was my biological father. It was late pre-emptive honesty. Her words simply confirmed what I somehow already knew.

I was four, sitting in the passenger seat of Mum's old blue Triumph Herald two-door convertible at the Hammersmith roundabout in London. I could just see over the cream mock leather sill. A green Rolls Royce hooted its horn, and she waved. I imagine it wasn't the coincidence I thought it was until now.

We drove into a Hilton. She and he sat opposite on blue velvet sofas; a large glass table in the middle kept them at their distance. I knew no boundaries; I leant on his knee, he looked at me intently, I feel this in my bones even now. They talked and we left. I never met him face to face again.

Two decades later I found Peter in Florida and a telephone number for his real estate business. She was keen on the idea, but I don't know why. He had fled from prosecution as the co-creator of the largest-ever Lloyds insurance heist.

I wanted to know some part of who created me. My naivety. I phoned him twice. Both conversations repeaters. "You're my father, I would like to know you. You have two wonderful grandchildren. I want nothing from you except to know you." I waffled to his cagey unresponsiveness, sweaty hands and armpits keeping my justification company, craving something back, not to beg for his acknowledgement. His response both times: "I will write to you. I will be in touch. Thank you for your call."

Liar and cheater — Lie and cheat.

He never wrote. I never heard. He'd paid my school fees and bought my first car, and that was it.

I swallowed it down. My habit…

Peter the Repeater walked away when the going got tough and he had to give something of himself, not money. I was the daughter he told no one about.

Wanker.

See Monday 10th March 1986's *Daily Mail* front page opposite…

EXCLUSIVE

FOUND: MISSING LLOYD'S TYCOON

From BRIAN VINE
In Warrenton, Virginia

THE Daily Mail has tracked down Peter Dixon, the fugitive Lloyd's underwriter accused of siphoning off more than £7 million in the greatest insurance scandal in the history of the City of London.

He is living in splendid luxury in one of the most exclusive areas of America—the heart of Virginia fox-hunting country.

But he says he will not return to London to pay the £1 million fine by Lloyd's imposed on him, because he has no money.

I interviewed him yesterday after seeing him standing on the terrace steps of his family's immaculately columned mansion. He was dressed immaculately in English blue blazer and slacks. Hunting dogs crouched at his feet.

'This house belongs to my wife,' he said. 'I have no funds of my own. I don't ride horses. I wander around behind the basset hounds, and you can make what you like of it all.'

'The High Court in London says he personally received £7.1 million in the PCW insurance syndicate scandal but he told me that he was under strict advice from his lawyer. 'I have been told not to litigate my affairs in the Press.'

He added : 'All these allegations have destroyed my life.'

But not, it would seem, his lifestyle. In America it is as high as it was in the heady days in London when he was regarded as a City wizard, with millions of pounds available for conspicuous personal consumption.

His style of living outside the old colonial town of Warrenton is that of a landed gentleman who with ted by the hunting squirearchy, and his abode with is set up like Scarlett O'Hara's of Gone With The Wind in a Tara-like pillared mansion.

PETER DIXON . . . living in luxury

Turn to Page 2, Col. 4

INSIDE: World Wide 10, Femail 12, Mail Diary 19, TV Guide 22, Ideal Home Exhibition 26, 27, Letters 30, City 32, Business to Business 32, 34, 35, Sport 35-40

EXCLUSIVE

Big shot Bruno in Las Vegas

THE Big Man is in town. Frank Bruno sets his sights on boxing's capital, Las Vegas, and meets the greatest. Full story : Centre Pages.
Picture by MONTY FRESCO

Bare Feet

He bought me shoes,
Dad,
My unsuspecting un-biological,
He let me choose,
She wasn't there,
And he didn't care
Between the booze.
They were brown and plastic,
With a heel
That looked like wood.
I felt so grown up,
Here comes my womanhood,
This bright, funny, free creature inside.
Mum took them away,
Gave them away,
To a little Irish lady named Marion,
Who was very, very little,
Only 4 ft 9,
She was taller in my shoes,
I was so very much smaller.

James

I struggle to write about my father:
All that our relationship seemed to contain was
His addiction.
It damaged three of his kids,
As for my brother (who became a half), I don't know, as we
never had an intimate conversation.
Fractured and distant as siblings.
It was what someone lazily called the Demon Drink
So flippant
D-evil lived in a whisky bottle and pint
Waved from the empty glass.
Forgetting lived there also.
I do not know what harmed him.
I did not know to ask.

He terrified me as a child. Saddened me as an adult.
Mum would deliver me to chaos.
The head fuck she had escaped.
I spent holidays in rooms of men propping up bars
Trying to escape something they maybe never knew.
Cricket clubs of male bravado, easy pray for some young
Lothario, an easy snog on a warm summer's night.
I went from mum the prison warder, to him the warder of a
bar stool.
He had no idea how to parent
I had no idea how to be his daughter
We were strangers, anaesthetised at the bottom of his
Numbing.

He was absent
I learnt numbing
It doesn't take alcohol
I never drink past two glasses
I am a cheap date.
I wonder if he knew
That she had lied
To us both.

"Daddy, I think I've got chicken pox!" I said, opening the top of my cotton blue nightie, a big girl at 8 to be going to the bar in a small pension we stayed in France when it was bedtime to show Dad the rash. The bar full of people, the smell of Provence wine, Pernod aniseed and voices filled the place. I forgot to read the signs.

He picked me up and turned me 180 degrees in a second. My face met ornate corners of the billiard table he had been leaning against, he held me by my ankles, my nightie around my neck, my body naked for everyone to see. "Let's see this rash!" he laughed.

I remember that I don't remember what they did about my eye. I remember watching it change a rainbow of colours. I remember sitting in the back of the car while he drove drunk, me so desperate to please, to survive chaos. I don't know if it was chicken pox.

MY BLACK EYE

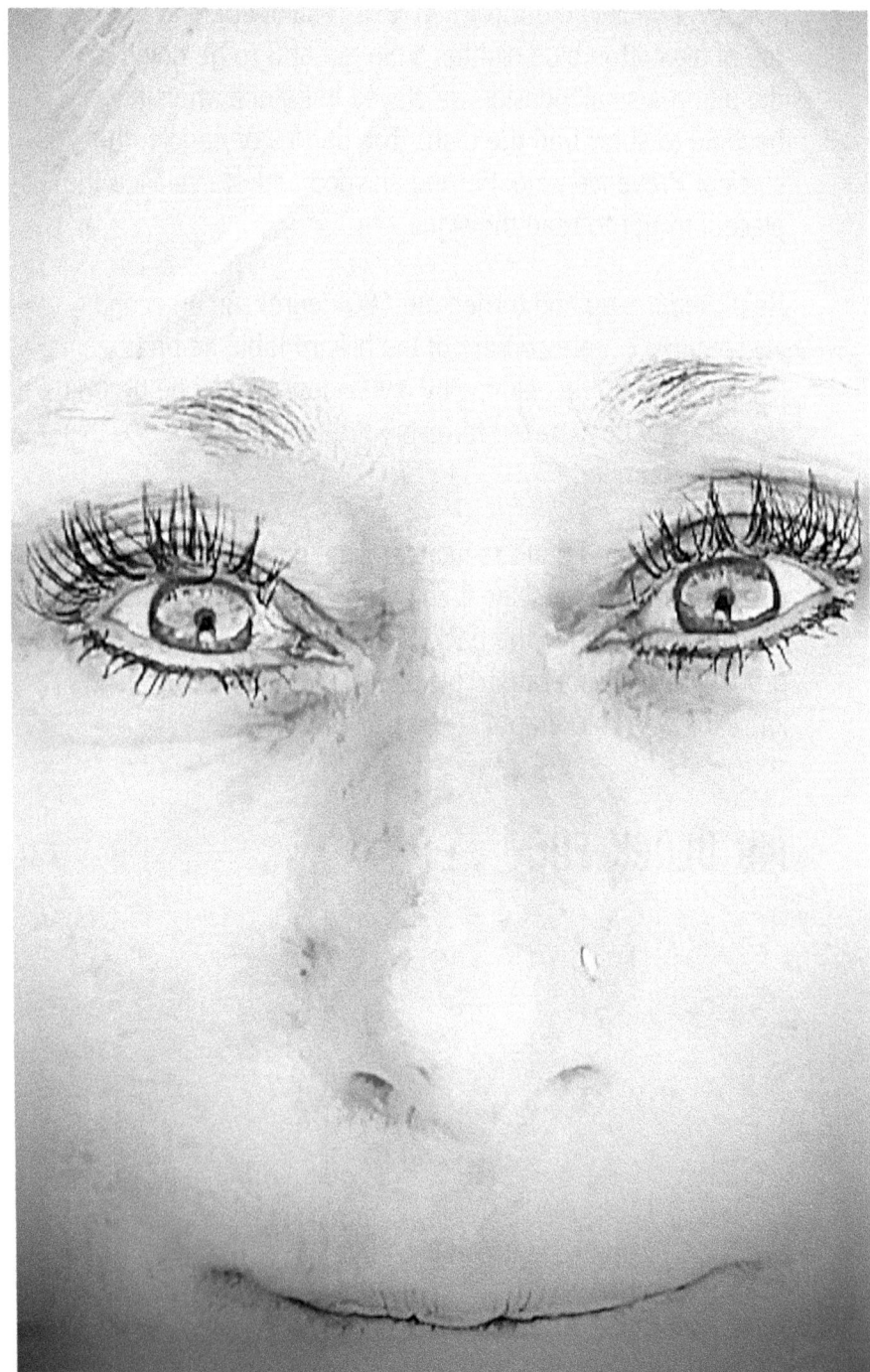

I LEARNT TO
PARENT AND
ADULT MYSELF
FROM CHAOS AND
WOUNDS.
SOMETIMES WELL.
SOMETIMES NOT. (THIS STILL APPLIES)

Dance Like No One is Watching

I was 15 and took myself out of boarding school to
Goldsmith University in London for a Performing Arts
Course audition without Mum's permission. I knew if I asked
beforehand there would be no audition, so I never did. I
have always been a dancer. I'd never had lessons. I danced
with girls who had been primed. I was not afraid.
I waited for the letter with hope.

The letter came, I was offered a place. The thrill tempered
with terror of having to ask my mother, but surely, she
would see how much this meant to me, she would know this
was huge.

She didn't, there was no discussion.

I went to Windsor and Eton Sixth Form College for a year's
Secretarial Course.
I learnt shorthand and typing.
I am the dancer who never got seen.
Invisible.

NOTHING HAS "MEANINGS" UNTIL THE MIND GET BUSY AND PUTS ONE TO IT.

CHAPTER 2

THE HURT

Mirrors

We lived in reactive behaviour. In ideas about how everything said something about us. Ideas about how everyone else didn't lack and we did. We should be different, more like someone else. Life lived in judgement.

We lived in ideas about how everyone else should treat us different. Ideas about competition, about how we would look to everyone else if we were or were not successful.

We lived in ideas about how we wanted it to be. Ideas how we wanted to be valued by others. Ideas about money and how we related to it. What our body said about us.

We lived in ideas about how everyone could be so cruel, a constant state of assessment that looked like everything and every person was the problem and how they made us feel.

We became adults with ideas.

We lived in submission to our mothers. The submissive needs a dominator; Mummy was a dominator, as was my grandmother.

We had different strategies.
She was always noisily right.
I was always silent,
Allowing survival of the narcissist.

We lived a plus and minus spreadsheet, our heads
SCREAMING,
"I did nothing here, it's all caused by them/that."

We had been taught by generations of learnings that we are
hurt by what's outside us.

I am not my psychology, but it is always my current novel

Believer

I viewed life through the lens of the ideas about me.
It's a self-fulfilling prophecy.

SeLF-HarMing

I am the victimised   daughter
of a victimised   daughter
Maybe my grandmother was too
I don't know
My   daughter
Was victimised by my victimising

                                                       mother

She tells me I don't victimise her
I've hugged her through her pain
I've held myself through mine
The only one I've victimised was

                                                       myself
I see my   daughter
Do it too
As a   victim
You turn it outwards
The external victimiser   bully
Or inwards
The internal victimiser   bully
It's destructive either way.

there is nothing
i havent
survived
even though i
thought i
couldnt

I AM STUPID

"You are fucking stupid," said Mummy. Her face unwrinkled at 80 from her facelift, now contorted with rage, her body encased in the voluminous blue velour zip-up dressing gown she always wore these days, size 28, tight, food stuck on it where her huge breasts acted as a bib. She sat on a dust-sheeted sofa strewn with papers. The ice-harsh fluorescent workman's light in the corner glared, revealing cold shadows. Her diamonds sparkled. The lounge walls naked except new pink wet plaster; it smelled musty. The floor a wooden puzzle of dusty footprints. Her bare feet were planted firmly, grey with dust. A crumpled ticket for the Eiffel Tower on the windowsill. She didn't travel. I could taste the plaster powder, my mouth vacant, dry and sticky. Damp blonde hair stuck to my neck. The dust in rivulets settled on my wet black shoes.

I hear incessant white noise raining outside. I can't hear my heartbeat inside me. I am empty, hollow, gouged. All I feel is the echo — loveless and lacking. I've always been here. "You've never fucking understood anything," Mummy said.

COME SIT WITH ME

"I'd like to go through my will. I know I am a long way off dying, but just humour me again. You've been a good daughter, though sometimes you haven't done what I wanted. Overall, you've been ok," Mum said and picked up the notepad, the pages, full of property names and assets, calculations of worth in the pot. Items ascribed to how much people mattered, how good they had been.
This list changed. Mostly it was about what my brother didn't get.

They were like strangers that passed in the night. She was vitriolic and hurt and he simply ducked out for most of his 50 years. Maybe he felt pushed aside by me being there, or maybe he was just free. I felt abandoned to have to be there solo, mixed with the feeling that I was important to her. I gave up trying to be their healer. Maybe it also filled my need to be picked.

Picked no matter how destructive it was. Being picked looks about love. Love was about money.

DEMONS HATE FRESH AIR

GREED

"I've changed my will," Mummy said. "William gets the majority." The hospital disinfectant aroma stung my nose, affronted by the chemical vapour. The plastic protector stuck out from the creased white pillowcase of the hospital pillow. Her unhampered hair wired around her oddly unwrinkled face. A face lifted 15 years earlier hid ugly unkindness. Her infected body swathed in her obligatory midnight blue velour zip-up Marks and Spencer's dressing gown. The harsh flickering fluorescent lights threw shadows of infusion across the white melamine floor. A&E cacophony paused. I stood rigidly grounded. Black soled trainers glued to the emergency room sticky history. Bags of puffy exhaustion hung under soulful hurt eyes. The first crack in my heart noticed. A blue jay feather stuck to the emergency button.

"You never understood," I said. "I was never here for the money."

Inside I heard, "Only what it said about me in your head."

Broke

I am jittered and jagged,
It descended last night like a cold shower,
A shower of discontentment washed through my cells,
A viscous scrub over of raw emotion,
I was looking at light fittings online at John Lewis,
I love doing things new,
Creating something of beauty,
I get bored of the same,
I like a challenge,
I am talented,
I fall flat on my face sometimes,
I search for a better me,
I am unworthy,
I am of no value.

My value was pounds, shillings and pence,
That's how she worked,
My lifetime of care for a narcissistic mother.
Exhausted and desecrated,
I craved her love and approval,
My brother's value for never being there,
Was written in words and observed by a solicitor,
I saw my value rated in the lack,
All I wanted was not to have a price,
She never said she loved me as she died,
I carry her price silently,
My invisible skin.
My underbelly.

I'M FINE

"I can't come home yet," I said, pained. "I'm at the park."

I carelessly discarded my phone to oblivion. I lay on sweet-smelling grass; a dusting of tiny blue flowers hid close to the ground. Above, the soldiers of blue pines cast silhouettes against the pure sky. White jeans and a blue shirt lay stuck to the warm earth. Toxicity seeped from my body; putrid energy absorbed. My fingernails clogged with dry soil scraped looking for healing. The yellow sun blazed my cold face; poisonous grief filled the hollow chambers. Breath paused on tinged blue lips.

"Excuse me, are you okay?" a woman I didn't know asked.

"Yes," I said.

I reeked of her and my brother's toxicity, not the hospital. I'd soaked it all up like a diaphragm taught to inhale, pervasive in every cell. I wanted to run and not to be at her death side again; my self-preservation told me to leave, not to be sucked dry by duty. I stayed keeping the twisted idea alive of what a good daughter does, no matter how annihilated she is.

SLasHer

She cut her arms in a bid of suicide, whilst nurses were busy, with a Victorinox kitchen knife. I have no idea why my brother bought it in. The hospital said no one outside the nutty ward had ever done this until my so-called sane unsane mother. The pit of my stomach I left at the ward entrance — it was safer there.

Drowning in Poison

Her lungs drowned in venomous poison,
She had come home to die,
Her choice to end it.
The poison that was in her heart,
Poisoned me too,
What her decision blatantly said about my lack.
The poison in her was more than bacteria,
It filled every cell,
Every thought,
In words she always vocalised,
No filter caressed her,
The cruel whip of her tongue,
Her love was lashed in my blood,
Splattered up my walls,
Dried, encrusted and stained.
I watched early in the dawn,
Aromatic and sweaty raised from sleep,
Sat on the hard wooden floor,
Buttocks numb from its unforgiving.
Slower, shallower fell her chest,
Slower, shallower my heart,
The most profound regret of love,
I couldn't breathe it into her,
The final breath of life left,
I felt it in my chest,
A snap of my heart,
For what had never been,
What never had a chance to be.

Her poisoned challis,
Drunk from so thirstily,
A life spat out to the world,
She spat no more.
Lying in her garden,
I vented a lifetime of grief,
For the mother,
I'd never had.
I washed her body,
Dressed her in clean M&S blue velour gown,
Cared and brushed her hair,
The most peace her body ever saw,
She wasn't there,
An empty circus,
A carcass unlived,
It just looked like my mother.

Looking For Love

My phone is beside me   the habit   I've got it in my head
to avoid it   It's a thing I long not to do   To not check
outside of me   When the day is so new.

    Love was not on her lips as she died.
    Emotionally crippled and needy, she lied.
    "I've been a good mother. I always tried."
    Love was not on her lips as she died.

I hate checking outside   It tells me all the shit that isn't
true   I need to be someone else   I need to be somehow
else   I need to be something else   It's got all the
answers to not being me.

    I waited inside for her outside,
    Just to tell me, "I love you,"
    It's a habit I'd like not to do.

Looking For Safety

I bumped into myself
This morning
In my bra drawer,
Dug through drawers of
Corpulent gluttony.
I'm enough
I hear myself wail
Just one more purchase
Will be plenty
To fill me up to enough,
And another
For just in case.
I'm not 'enough' enough
My poison of self-soothing
That hit of pleasure
And guilt
So tightly tagged
Together.
Lack is insatiable
I bumped into myself
In 34G
This morning,
Saw my pattern
Keeping me safe.

A CHILD OF LACK WILL ALWAYS NEED MORE

UN-LABELLING

I felt hate,
I felt relief,
I felt pain,
I felt space,
I felt me,
I felt bruised,
I understood baggage,
I love,
I heal,
I am unlabelled as daughter.

one year Later

The undertaker
Left her ashes
On my doorstep
In a blonde wooden box,
A gold plaque denoted
Patricia Joyce Crowley
1930 to August 2016.
She was stored in the shed
For many months
Where to scatter her?
Brother unbothered.
I took her to her affluent past
Virginia Water Lake
A bright summer day
Full of dog walkers and prams.
The box too obvious
I slipped her ashes into
A 5p Tesco carrier bag
Only a dusting on the car floor.
I meandered paths
Heart thumping
Slid eventually to the water's edge
And slipped her in.
A grey suspended film of dust
Nothing more
She floated for a little while.
I'm sure I heard her laugh
The slapstick would have amused her

I wished her farewell.
The blonde wooden box
I dropped in the recycling bin
I'm sure somebody wondered
Who and where was
Patricia Joyce Crowley
But might have guessed
Her final resting place.

RECYCLE(D) STARDUST

CHAPTER 3

MESSY STUFF LIVING

I LIVE FROM MY SCARS UNTIL I KNOW BETTER

Leader Table

I wait   the competitive school-gaters descend on cue
Women of "who has and does what" claws   They ski
every year   Holiday to the South of France for the summer
together
I'm insecure, and they terrify me   I say I don't want to be
in   Irritatingly inside   I want a crew   Occasionally even one
I don't really like
My kids are friendly and polite   Though secretly want to be
cool   They think they lack   Sometimes, I wish they were
cool too
The end of sanity   who's in and out
All the cool will be cold-shouldered one day
Fuck, what a shock   Life plays it that way
I'll wait until they're gone
I don't crave cool today.

I BLEW UP an ALFa ROMEO

I am paper-thin and fragile, like ancient parchment that
needs tender touch from gloved hands to not tear and
disintegrate. I feel like a nutter. An empath, I feel deeply my
world. Others seem oblivious to how they hurt.

My best friend left my son out of a birthday event. I barely
stood and said my farewells at the school gate, inside
me volcanic and feral, simply lived. Every cell filled with a
charge. I made it to the car, sat in the driver's seat and
screamed, screamed, screamed, screamed some more until
my throat silenced itself. My face savage and creased, I fired
the car and floored the accelerator, moved 20 feet and the
engine made a loud bang and stopped. It probably saved
my life.

I am a canvas.
Life is art.
I live the art of
thought.

SHIT AND THE FAN

Angry.
Lost.
Unhappy.
Fear.
Numb it.

THE FUCK GROOVE

I've given up,
I'm not doing that again.
Hmmmmm, my craving.
I've eaten four hobnobs dunked in very sweet tea,
I sat down to write, and fuck, it's worse,
The association between a fag and writing,
That quiet head space in zombie towers.
The pit in my stomach says this is what we do.
The addictive noise in my head is screaming and pacing The
corners of the room,
Beautifully attired in black Prada,
Addictions expensive,
She won't look me in the eye; she's furious,
She's muttering under her breath,
What the fuck, What the fuck, continuously.
She's engraving a groove in my synapses,
The Fuck Groove of:
What's going to be the next great idea.
The conversation goes:
Oh my god, she could give up her addiction to clothes And
shoes,
No, not shoes,
She'd never go there,
That's where she always goes when she's feeling lost,
Unhappy, doesn't know what else to do,
Shows she is as stupid as her mother said,
The conversation never ends.
Thank God, Prada to the rescue, Ferragamo's new season,

My Fuck Groove has been filling shelves for decades,
Boxes of fuck all over the place,
My synapses are very well connected,
The Fuck Groove is self-soothing,
The nicotine craving is right in my face,
Spitting saliva all over my makeup,
The shoes are something more profound, darker and
Needy,
Something so hidden I don't notice it,
It's quietly insidious and vaguely sad,
No spitting saliva, no slamming doors,
Not in my face at all,
But shoes have far more craving attached.

THE SOUL OF AVOIDANCE

I'm avoiding my heart,
I've it packed up and hidden it down in my toes,
No one will even think to look for it there,
It can keep doing its circulating thing,
But toe caps in all my shoes will keep it untrodden.
Sweet, pretty shoes are my protection,
That are rock-hard under the glamour,
They are keeping all my love safe,
Laces of feelings occasionally climb up to be snipped and
tightly retired,
I'm safer like this,
Far fewer blisters, no corns or swelling.
I am a parade of stilettos on the outside,
Wedges are like blocks on an aeroplane wheel, stopping my
Heart from freedom,
My trainers keep me running from all the confusion of
Sharing loving,
Wellies keep the poison out and me in.
My heart is artfully buckled and encased in leather,
Free in the dark of sleep,
No expectations as to how it should feel,
No steel toe caps are provided,
This human heart thing can hurt,
Be battered, bruised and imaginatively broken,
I've felt it crack, a razor-sharp shard,
Get lost in my chest,
That sometimes tries to walk its way out
Of being enmeshed in my toes

Under manicured nails and pink enamel.
I work so hard to keep balanced,
Toes are severely underrated,
As the place of choice,
For the protection of a very tender heart that
Wants to know it's safe to love back.

LaBeLS

My
diagnosing,
pricing,
behaviour,
in and out thing,
value,
My
definition of me,
good and bad of anything,
problem,
solution,
this is a good day,
this one is a shit day,
My
lack of,
much of,
the right and the wrong,
I'm successful,
I'm not,
the place that I live,
places I don't,
My habits,
idiosyncrasies of how I relate to the world,
am I hot or not,
my rich or my poor,
disciplined or not,
fear or fearless,
marital status,

colour of skin,
My
star sign,
spiritual or decadent,
an influencer or influenced,
learner or teacher,
a rebel with or without any cause,
I would like to be like them but not like them;
Thank you.
Family,
society
status
Labels that incapacitate
Say something,
About being
Me.

everyone needs

Broken teacups of delicate china
                              Two feet to stand   on
The   quiet
  I   rescue   being me
voiceless   Drown in
 Seas of salty waves   I   survive
In   kindness I am   loved
                              Love exists
And
Damp grass stains my knees   Healer, heal thyself
I fall down   the rabbit   holes in the garden
            I have a suitcase   big   enough
 everyone else's shit   I'm strong

Whoever shouts   loud   enough gets my   attention
Can anyone hear me?
 the sticking plaster for everyone's needs
Loves kisses are my reward
                              I've forgotten
    Me, I   blessed

THERE ARE NO RULES – read this in whatever order you wish

THIS IS YOUR PAGE... WHAT NO RULES WANT TO BE HEARD FROM YOU?

CLUTTER OF WORRY

My head is stretched,
I live in what might happen.
My body is broken.
A pained mind evokes my pained body.

My body stopped
Took me to surviving,
Unable to function,
To switch off my stress,
Not my choosing, despite it,
Laid me to bed,
Put me to sleep.
I was a hermit living under a duvet,
Where worry became elusive,
My children survived
Stuff didn't get done,
The world didn't end.

WHICH THERAPY TODAY? I'M SICK

Sick in the head.   Psychotic madwoman.
Should be happy.
    That's what it said.   The voice in my head.
Everything looks rosy.
    I have a dark cloud.   It's curled up inside.
Someone help me.
    Sign me up.   Get it removed.
I'll pass it to you.
    History.   Future.
Learnings.
    It's not me.   It takes me over.
I'm powerless.   That's what it says.

ADVICE

Sandy told me I was bored. She can read people, so she said. Warm coffee and garlic flowed the air around us. A newborn baby out to lunch cried for her mother's breast. Women nattered. Glasses clinked. We sat in green velvet chairs at a low table. Sandy was so sure and convincing. Who knew? Clearly not me. Advice is so helpful or not when you think you can see inside someone's head.

THE WRONG MATHS

Inside my head — she didn't smile back & she saw me
EQUALS
She doesn't like me
I'm not important
I think she's jealous
I am not worthy
She thinks I'm fat and feels sorry for me
I'm not cool
Just how rude
I'll ignore her later
What did I say?
Oh my god I will never speak to her again
I bet she is up to something.

Back story

Two hours earlier her best friend had been diagnosed with breast cancer. She was sad.

Everything was added up wrong.

THE WORLD ISN'T AN
ILLUSION
BUT I LIVE IN
ILLUSIONS ABOUT THE
WORLD

Tailoring

I am a woman of personas
All with immaculate stitching
Impressively lined
Beautiful haute couture to fit.
I have a wardrobe of Me's on padded hangers
The pink linen one is for my sassy mood
A blue pinstripe for the serious stuff of business
The yellow floral one, rarely worn now, is the controlled Wife
That one I designed,
I have a floaty red one for motherhood with many pockets
A black itchy suit for my daughterhood
That has a snag up the sleeve,
The revealing yellow halter-neck trouser suit
Is the one for the writer I wear a lot now,
Blue polka dots fit the mood of the creator of social media.
I tuck at the back, but it often sneaks out
The polyester bobbled midnight blue one of insecurity And
victim
My favourite one is the purple silk slink of fuck it,
I go through phases with that one.
There are dozens more
Some the moths have eaten discreetly
They just haven't been destroyed
They might still do a turn,
Like the emperor's new suit
Invisible but here in my head.
Some I've inherited and tailored to fit

Others I've willingly adopted with a pinch and a nip
Others newly imagined,
Each one has a different subliminal sown into the hem
I like the nuances of details only the experienced eye Would spot.
I have an unseen tailor and designer of my unique Messiness
It's invisibly neat and very talented.

SOMETIMES IT JUST DOESN'T WORK

I dislike her vibe,
Tried good thoughts,
Lighting candles and asking for wisdom,
The idea of her is nails on a chalkboard
Or a wooden spoon on my tongue,
We don't fit,
We hide it so well
With social pleasantries,
Each looking over the other's shoulder,
For anyone that would be more conducive,
Everyone else.
Clearly, I'm not seeing the oneness below,
She reminds me of my mother,
Slags everyone off,
Then face to face sweet as ice and a slice,
It sticks like a claw.
I hate being fake,
I want to say,
Fuck off, you two-faced cow.

Being spiritual is
a lifestyle
choice -
Being spirit isn't
optional

CHAPTER 4

THE UNSEEN

THE VEIL

I was taught there was something between me and the "other" world.

There isn't.

Unagreed Haunting

Her skin moulded to mine,
She invaded for a while,
My mother.
I disappeared,
Her sallow, stretched skin in the mirror,
She always stared back dead.
She haunted without permission.
She slipped in unseen,
Whilst I was deep in healing,
When I was looking elsewhere,
When I thought she'd gone with her body,
She got lucky,
I wasn't.
She passes by, but I know her now,
She isn't ever getting in again.
Stay dead in ether.
What you missed, you can't have now.

HOW I AM WIRED

I had a visit, a man full of light, his name he told me was Jesus. We had a conversation. I can't remember it now. You'd imagine I would. I know it was important. I attend to children and adults unseen for moments of healing or love. Premonitions of future unknown events, things I can't change. I watch them humdrum unfold, life savers and intuition. Losing a bracelet, I knew to water. I didn't think it would be down the toilet. Darker energies visit and disturb my equanimity; they linger, the blackest molasses. I sponge up people's sadness and trauma, their laughter and joy.

My hands in someone else's body healing with tinkering and stitches. The most profoundly beautiful gift holding my babies' hands whilst still in my womb. Ghosts in my home. The woman whose dark clothes and unclear face travels each house move seems to have packed herself up.

Spirits in my body. This energetic psychic, unknown yet known world, that I have no choice in how it shows itself to me. Leaves me nakedly exposed and vulnerable. No ownership of how it turns up. A whole spiritual energetic world that enthrals me. I live vigilant, acceptance of no boundary, many intrusions and blessings. I am a witch, and I don't like stakes.

Human Hurts

My wings hurt,
Tied up so tightly,
Restricted and immobile,
Invisible to the eye,
Sitting at the junction of my blades,
I am their feathered magnificence,
Unfurled,
I dance the winds,
But earthly responsibilities,
Constrict,
The unseen symbol of my spirit,
Deeply embedded,
They rub where my skin erupts,
Into my humanness,
There before I was born,
I struggle with the before and the after,
Weighed down,
Windless I remain.
Tied to gravity,
Happiest when I fly,
Stuck on the ground is stuck,
If I put down the sack full of tat,
And let them be seen,
No need to hide,
No need to fit in,
In a world of
Need to be normal,
No need to toe the imaginary line,

The tale of womanhood,
Daughter, mother, wife,
My spirit has no gender,
No skin and wings.

I am creation.
I am eternal.

conversationing with the dead

7th of June early am, Husband quietly snoring I sipped my hot tea. Watching the skittish rabbits, silently collecting the moment.

He appeared next to the bed, a hunched, half-bald white-haired man holding his head in pained expression.

I couldn't tell you if we spoke words,

Or if it was in our heads.

He asked what had happened. He remembered bumping his head then nothing, until me.

So very confused, so very lost.

I answered in words that were silent, I think, that I was pretty sure he had passed away and, in the shock, he had lost his way into an illusion of life.

I watched his face rest amongst the creases.

"Can you see somewhere to go?" I asked. "Could you just let go?"

I watched him settle a smile in something he recognised.

I silently cried at the beauty as he disappeared like the morning haze as the sun rises,

Or smoke from a dwindling fire that the breeze takes away.

He went home, where we all go one day. Where we come from.

Somewhere unseen.

Dearly Departed

Today at Pilates I felt someone who I used to know, she passed away a decade or so ago. I knew who it was, I can feel her still. Sue was her name. A nice ordinary woman with slightly protruding teeth and a sprinkling of freckles, dark hair and long fingers. She wore dowdy clothes at the school gate, like a vicar's wife. Sue stood in that slightly folded-in kind of way, shirts with a frilly collar under a navy-blue jumper. A skirt that looked like an ill-fitting bag and something sensible on her feet. She had two boys. One in my son's class. I can't remember now if there was a daughter. A husband called Harry. One night she went to sleep and never woke up. No one got to say goodbye, or I love you. I think that's why she is here today and sits with me now. Maybe she'll tell me what she wants. Harry got remarried a few years later. Maybe she is just lonely today. She felt younger today than I remembered her, but I am older.

A VISITOR I DON'T MIND THESE DAYS

She, Mum, comes often these days. I'm not frightened of her visits. She's changed and so have I. I know her like a sixth sense; part of a carpet, we are woven together. She comes when I'm with my kids, like the important things she missed she wants to touch, or the laughter with girlfriends she'd forgotten in the ending. Mum asked for forgiveness on a sun-bleached decking in Colorado with a psychic called Karen, who didn't know our journey together.

"I have learnt what love is. I had to come here to know. Please can you forgive me?'

Karen repeated her words.

I lied and said "Yes."

Healing took a little longer.

PLATFORM PSYCHIC

The final day of a week course "Art and Mediumship" at Arthur Findlay College. The night previously I had sat in the dark on this stage, alone except for the October full moon filtered through the stained-glass windows of the sanctuary, I heard the laugher and chatter of my course mates in the bar. I cried to my three parents all the anger in my heart at their shitty parenting and scars that had tortured our time. I shouted to my mother the pain she caused my kids, especially my daughter, undeserved. I spoke the things that I had never got to tell them in life, words I wanted to be rid of.

I stood now waiting for who wanted to be heard that couldn't be seen. My hair scooped up in a clip, freed itself in straggled pieces, blue hippy trousers finished above silver ankle bracelets, white linen top and a wool cardigan of knitted rainbow colours. The sun warmed the room from the south-faced garden windows and lit the floating dust. I waited, breathed slowly and settled my feet to the ground silently.

"I have 3 people here, but they are mine and they want to share their truth," I said. They stood slightly behind me off to my right. "We are all lost children. We spend our time frightened of it, what a waste of our time," I said, tears welled as my heartbeat deepened. "Don't be afraid — it is essential. It is part of what we are designed for, you are safe."

I spoke their words as Cory sat in the front row leaned forward, tears rolling down his cheeks. The room silent. "You are safe, always have been, but it's time to know you're not that child now. You are loved and infinite."

Their words.

seen IT ALreaDy

I nudged forward slowly to the main road from the car park, the lights were green. I sat in the driver's seat on soft cream leather. Liz, my friend in the passenger seat, hesitated to put her seat belt on and waved to Anne, the friend we have both known for 30 years, who walked along the pavement towards my window, I tapped the brake to stop, ignoring my green light.

I turned to watch her walk slowly smiling in a farewell wave, we had had a lovely lunch at the Weyside Pub in the sunshine. I could still taste lunch, garlic prawns and a small pink gin and tonic. A flash of blue Toyota shot past my bonnet. We felt the whoosh of speed passing inches away as my lights turned red. Liz, white-faced, clasped my arm and said,

"Georgia, he would have killed us."

"Don't worry – last night the car was red and he didn't kill us then either."

Patience

I stood naked in front of the mirror, black round hairbrush wound up with my blonde hair.
"Something's coming, wait," I heard.

MUM was a WITCH TOO

She phoned one morning.

"Go visit your mother now, something's wrong," she said to Philip, my husband, on a bleak day to come. Betty Iris, my mother-in-law, had a new knee that was causing her problems in hospital recovery. Betty Iris and my mother didn't talk. By the time my husband got to the hospital, Betty Iris, his mother, had exited this life, so sadly.

My mother was psychic — she thought it was all rubbish, cults and woo-woo.

I beg to differ.

It terrified her.

unDressing

CHAPTER 5

LOSS

IN-SIGHT – a recognition in my awareness that shifts a knowing of expanded truth. A ripple through space of remembering.

I am
Awareness and light
The being before the thoughts
The oneness of the watcher
Who views the screen
Of life.

TIME COMES TO
CHANGE THE
generational
narrative... IT'S
NOT CHOSEN BY
LITTLE OLD ME

"IT'S TIME," I HEARD

I woke up Wednesday night at 3am, in a half-built house, with a seriously ill daughter, deeply stressed, tired and heard, "It's time to learn something." Pottered through to the cement-floored kitchen, past the temporary shower in the hall, brushed the dust off the sofa, opened Google. I asked it *'Kinesiology? or Acupuncture?'* By 4 am was signed on to a Kinesiology course that started on Saturday. The learning began following intuition and feel. I don't know I had a choice.

Psych-K® next — how the body holds and shows answers to "knowing" in my body/mind. Change a negative belief to a good one, just change your mind. I witnessed a miracle in someone I hold so dear. The pause and exploration into how life simply looked to them through their filters. Divinely guided to be there, the flow of my life changed, my intuition sharpened. I had to lose me to find me.

I looked inside and asked, *Where am I*, here in this filing system of join the dots, brain, nerves, neurons and cells, bone and membranes. It's all biology, chemistry, physics and electricity — none of it named Georgia.

I got turned inside out by a book *The Inside-Out Revolution* by Michael Neill, and nothing's been quite the same since. I still have my husband and family, I live in the same house, I still walk my dogs and hate housework (so much else I'd rather be doing!), I lost parts of what was there and found something else that had been there the whole time. So, it's been loss, stripping, getting naked and fuck, can it be uncomfortable, vulnerable and raw. I've felt safer for losing and loving me.

Be brave, devote yourself to you. It is the place where you get to know you are not what you think, and you are whole, always were. Like me.

I QUESTIONED

I think

They are not the same.

I know

LOSE YOURSELF IT'S IMPERATIVE TO FINDING YOU

♥

sorry is simple

I found this picture in old stuff when she died. This smile I don't remember when I was old enough to recall. My memories, sharp and vitriolic with each year older. Hurt people hurt people. I am a child who never spoke up, a pleaser of people, a trait I try hard not to fall into these days. Sometimes it's hard and I miss my preset until I'm in so deep, it's choking me like old vines that never give up. I taught my children to please other people – I wish I knew better in the past. I was a teacher of my internal dialogue. I've since apologised.

SHE CALLED

"Come into the wilderness,"
I heard her call,
What awaits is not known,
It's full of possibilities,
Of treasure and truth.
She called from deep inside,
A haunting arose,
Each cell responding to the rhythm,
A slow melodic beat that rippled like the tide.
So, I ran into the wilderness,
Bohemian without regard,
To the space where there is nothingness to behold,
And there I found not knowing,
Blissful in its caress,
A possibility,
No past,
No future,
Now.

Genius Catalyst

A great teacher awaited,
He didn't know me.
It takes some courage,
To start,
To blindly follow,
And sometimes
No courage at all.
My teacher said 'Fuck' a lot,
Maybe that's why I like him,
I say 'Fuck' a lot too.

DON'T DO FAINT-HEARTED

"Look under the façade of what you think you are," said Wyn, my coach.

A tear rolled gently down the trough of makeup beautifully arranged on my tanned skin. My blue eyes wandered off the Zoom computer screen. The desk in front of me scattered with crisp white paper with scribbled neat handwriting, meaningful quotes, things to do, ponderings, and things to instruct, inspire, inform or ignite me. Pens strewn across the grey wool carpet that Jac, my rescue jackdaw, had stolen and abandoned, nibs crushed, and lids tucked behind pillows. On the cream sofas lay my dogs, twitching in sleeping dreams of chasing rabbits and such. A garlic clove tucked securely in the edge of the seat I sat on between the cushion and arm, a donation from Jac (he steals).

"I am frightened to not be the me I think I am," I said quietly.

Wyn silently looked back and sipped his ginger and fennel green tea.

Beneath all the layers of my 'so sure', knowing about what and who I am, my limitations, my back story, and my abilities, is nothing. An empty void un-full of my story. The tale created by my upbringing, years of surviving narcissism, my ego, my looks, my society, the books I've read, the habitual noise in my head. In the void, none of it looked true in the façade of me. Without the frontage, nothing was known or set.

Absolutely terrifying.

Praying (Ode to Michael Neill)

A quietness sitting inside, always waiting.
I stop for a moment,
Breathe and settle back,
Not with what's in the mirror.
I saw it, in a moment, in someone else.
I nearly choked my lunch,
God, without any viewed presence,
Flowed through his physical form.
From somewhere not defined.
Unearthed, unsolid, unfathomably immense.
It lived him.
I ask for guidance in prayer.
Conversations with my essence gets quiet.
Sometimes I forget.
When I remember I discover myself all over again.
The immenseness that lives me.
I close my eyes and have a natter with the universe.
We are lived by the same thing.

Naked

Source

Universal Intelligence

Divine Energy

Gut Feel

Inner Voice

Intuition

Hunch

Energy

Spirit

The Trilogy

Mind

Wisdom

Something Bigger than Me

Invisible Divine Intelligence

Woo-woo Stuff

The Supreme Being

The Controller

The Creator

A Deity

Ruler of the Universe

The Omnipresence of All Things

She

El

Lord

Something Unknowable but Felt

Allah

Brahman

Krishna-Vasudeva

The All

The Voice

Creative Genius

The Flow

Life

God

Love

Please take your pick of one or all of these for something bigger than the label of a word. You get to choose.

HFMOG

When I am six feet under
I'll wonder why it took me so long
To get the cosmic joke,
Thinking just isn't mine,
I just heard the same thought as you
In the flavour of me,
Just maybe not at the same time.
Plainly speaking,
It's an illusion,
It's just like the air
Nothing about the bit that I inhale
Is anyway personal,
The script and the atmosphere aren't about me,
I am an audience and an inhaler.

holyfuckingmotherofgod

TRUTH

Your brain lies constantly – The unreliable narrator.
Your avoiding "uncomfortable" gives it control.
Your identity isn't fixed.
Your wired for emotion, but built to regulate it.
Your suffering means your human. Choose it wisely.
Your grief means you've Loved.

My brain lies constantly – My unreliable narrator.
My avoiding "uncomfortable" gives it control.
My identity isn't fixed.
My system is wired for emotion and built to regulate it.
My suffering means I am human. I chose wisely.
My grief means I've Loved.

WHO IS BATTLING
THE THOUGHT
THAT ISN'T
COMFORTABLE?

(SPOILER ALERT –
THE SAME MIND)

I DISAPPEARED IN THE SHOWER

I have a thought.
It says
Be frightened to shine,
Everything will change,
Life will be blown apart,
Stick in a comfort zone in ideas of mediocrity.
I wait to see what's behind and, in my humanity,
Something spectacular that I just know is there,
Life's been fighting to be seen,
I thought the inner knowing wasn't about Georgia.

I stepped into the shower and turned the stainless dials left; hot water deluged in crystal-softened droplets. The garden beyond the window was veiled through opaque damp glass. Jac, my jackdaw, silhouetted on the window ledge. Hazed steam filled the space, and I stood in the hot flow. Naked, my blonde hair with dark uncoloured roots, skin suntanned with the vague remains of untanned buttocks. Older skin wetly drenched unnoticed. Nipples brownly erect from the cold air. Warm air cloudy, meeting cold hung suspended. The large unframed bathroom mirrors a patchwork of fingerprints. In an ordinary moment I ended nowhere, not in the room, not in the universe. I'd disappeared into what I am, the energy life. The hugeness of what I am before everything, being a human. I started and ended nowhere just for a moment or three.

I laughed and cried vaguely manic
Tears of sadness for the wasted, laughter of joy unfettered,
Tears for the love, laughter at the unknown absurdity,
Dropping to the floor in utter mind-blown amazement.

I had no idea about me,
I disappeared,
And expanded,
The safest I've ever been,
No shining brighter to ever have to do.
No giving up to do.
I was the brightest thing there is.
The deepest vibrating enormity of disappearing
to emerge as me
In a whole different way, suddenly existed.
It wasn't about Georgia, but it was.

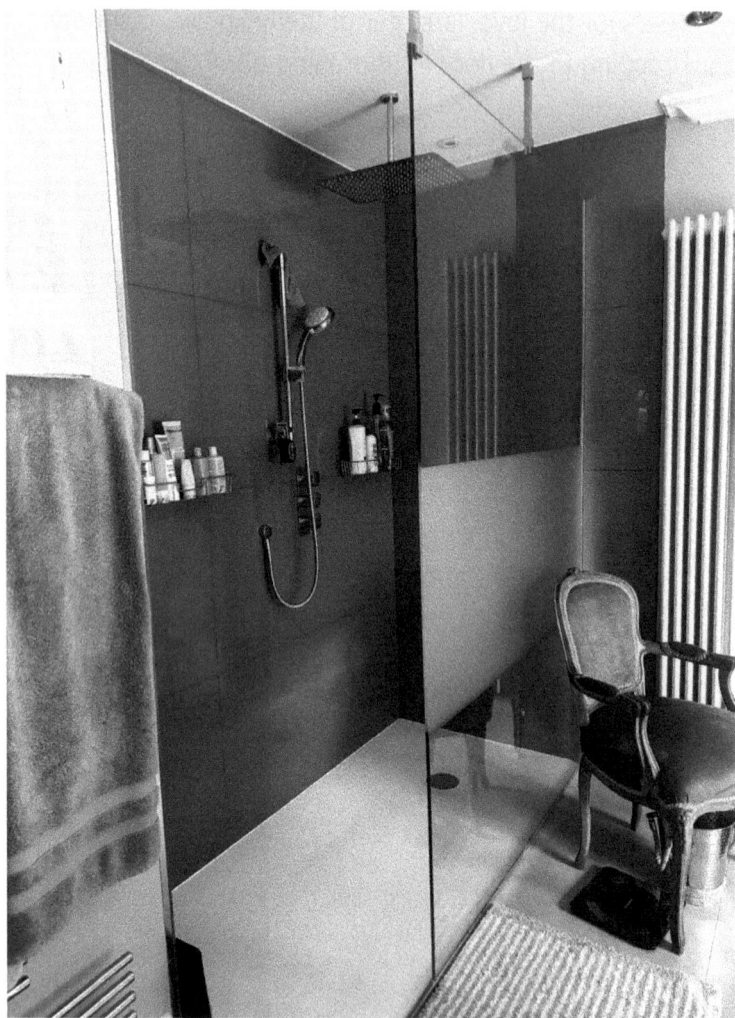

LIFE CHANGES ANYWHERE

HEALING THE CHILD

I see an osteopath; Sam is her name. I trust when to see her. In the process of writing this book I've seen her often. As I write the memories out, my body needs the same release of what's sat in its cells.

I lay on the treatment bed, Sam's hands on my head and I was back as a child with a stranger's hand on my head, doing something I didn't understand, an overwhelming feeling of being lost. I haven't touched that moment in a long time so closely.

I remember smiling at him, he'd talked to me often during our stay. Now he's just a faceless presence of no detail, other than he wasn't old. I remember him taking my hand and leading me along. I'd like to say I thought it was a game — I don't have that clarity now. The encounter and being told to keep the secret quiet. I have lived with the story that it must have been me. It wasn't abuse because I didn't fight, I didn't scream, I didn't tell anybody — so I must have been complicit, maybe the instigator — did my childish smile say something? We learn masks as children around adult behaviour. I remember feeling grown up and pretty in the borrowed dress that day.

I have never felt angry, I have felt guilt and disgust. I was just as wrong as my story. I have had no ability to take a compliment, without closing the hatches down. As I grew up and I learnt to have ideas about me and what happened, I couldn't see the truth.

I was a child.

He was a paedophile.

It took me to being 60 to tell another person about it. I still don't know how to talk about it with ease, maybe that will come. I can't look back and comprehend from here, now. I have nothing rational to offer it. But trying to rationalise will always keep me in mind games. This is how abuse works in the mind. Why so many have no ability to talk about it — there is nothing rational in abuse. There is nothing rational in it being my fault.

Being at fault is a habit learnt. The only healing is understanding something deeper and honest conversations. It has said something about me all my life — keep quiet and sweep it under the edge of the rug where no one else can see the pile of dirt except my mind. As I find me, these lessons and experiences lose their ability to disempower me. It cannot define me unless I believe it does.

I know very few women who have not experienced some form of sexual abuse either themselves or their near ones. It's a quiet pandemic that relies on silence and mind games of self-blame and thinking we are safe from judgement if not spoken about, but there is an inner world of self-judgement that insidiously harms more.

The veil of consciousness creates a tissue paper lens, distorting reality only seen clearly through the rips. I'll never know the truth, the meaning, the 'why'. The only thing I know and will whisper 'til the end, **it was wrong.**

"PONDERING" BY FERRI FARAHMANDI,
THE SCULPTURE PARK, FARNHAM

ROLODEX

I misunderstood,
I have a label my mother chose
From some woman she liked.
My mind has a file called
Georgia
And another named
Mum.

WHOever said THIS AWAKENING STUFF'S EASY, WAS LYING

So many things I should be doing and don'ting,
Do build an empire,
Don't let it be about you,
Do stay young,
Don't do it from ego,
Do the Darling,
Do it because you're love,
Do chirpy without shit in the corner,
Don't do volatility or madness,
Do peace and love,
Do the teacher who doesn't teach,
Do simply show.
Do the curious questioner with no me involved,
Do the being of everything but as nothing,
Don't do the façade,
Do know what the façade is.
Do play as infinity whilst walking this plane,
Don't play the game of life from what I think,
Do play it from somewhere deeper,
Do discern the different voices,
Don't forget one is thinking intellect and one's spirit,
Do the work and the journey,
Don't forget no one needs fixing,
Do enjoy living, all of it,
Don't get caught up in any one part of it,
Do let anything I think flow by,

Do get curious about what doesn't flow by,
Don't forget there is always a lesson,
Do the doing of the energy of love impersonally,
Do fully relish and get intimate with all your pain,
Don't forget your pain is self-made,
Do live like the Buddha,
Do only love and service,
Do the tears, laughter, orgasms and tendonitis equally,
Don't forget to be vulnerable in a world that judges,
Do not be a judger,
Do the wise human who knows there is no doing to do,
Don't tell you this; let you see for yourself,
Do know when there is something to do that's inspired,
Don't do the doing but don't not,
Do the learning, not for the fixing,
Do know none of it's about me,
Do the branding without losing yourself,
Don't be me too much,
Don't say fuck,
Do be a colour palette; the market gets that,
Do be me but not the ethereal, people won't understand,
Do meet people at their level of consciousness,
Don't forget you know what that is innately,
Do the shouting quietly,
Don't do it complicated; keep it simple,
Don't treat people like they are idiots,
Don't intellectualise it,
Don't listen to the words, yet listen; that's all that's helpful,
Don't do being — just be,
The spiritual conditioning idea files.

Sometimes it is overwhelming…

I see you ugly

I've seen you,
The ugly, shrivelled copiously obese monster I believed was
me,
I see you, the nature of your snake-like skin, chameleon and
elusive,
You slithered in my arterial veins,
I see you,
I thought you were real, I had a picture of darkness,
I see you,
You seeped pungent from every pore, blocked me with
stench.
Afraid that all to be seen was a vile me,
I'd ask myself, "What's inside that I can't see?"
The one that's rotted and corroded, the Ugly me,
I saw you.
Your perimeter of caging disappeared in the blink of a
waking eye,
I see you,
Behind you,
What had been made up in the illusion of judgement,
There was no ugly, Ugly me was just you,
I see you,
Ugly had an energy of its own
I recognised the feel,
I hadn't seen that
You had première tickets, a royalty box for one,
I see you,
There is no need to hide, I am the light of no prison walls,

Nothing broken,
I see you,
I am not
ugly at all.

THE BURIAL

The fucker says:
I am enlightened,
I have a superpower,
One that sets me apart,
I'm ahead,
I am special.
All ego mind pillow talk.
I love the fucker when I spot it,
It's brilliant
I hate it when I don't —
Magnificent, isn't it
The more I question what's true,
The fucker gets unveiled.
I'm a fucker shooter,
No blood will be shed,
Fucker hides in the feel,
When fucker comes out to feed,
Fucker's dead
With the truth.

A grave mistake.

HI, I'M EGO

The one she called Fucker,
I am preferences, resistance and opinions,
Ideas of who you are,
A component to a 3D experience,
You can't write me off,
Or bury me under the patio.
I am vapid and shallow,
Heroic or slayer,
Malleable and changeable,
The flavours of you.
I am a concoction of stories and fables,
I am addressed as your ego,
I make everything personal.
I am so not yours,
Though I am you,
I'd have you believe,
I am all the creations that flow in your head.
I make you tight,
Control is my forte,
I go everywhere with you,
I'll never shut up,
I'm heard in the words
Felt in angsty feelings
That knock around,
I am all the shit and fantastic,
You think about yourself.
Fickle, easily blamed, hated or loved,
I lie,

I use HD to create you,
A picture of you and the world
In your head,
I label you in ideas of individual,
I am very proud of the millions of addictions
That look intimately owned,
I tell you they are.
I am a masterful creator,
Layers and layers that go together,
For the exquisite tasting of you.
I am you but I'm not,
I bear you no malice,
I like you safe, frightened and limited,
I was created from childhood, a primeval brain with
flavourings,
I make up shit,
I'm a joker,
I am created but not by you,
I'm not personal at all,
But we are intimate -
Deal with it.

Love Ego x

EGO ON TOUR

ADDICTION AND ANXIETY

Some of the most confident-looking people I know are terrified inside, propping themselves up with something. When I don't know what to do or how I feel, I shop, I'm self-soothing. Like dragging on a fag or a glass or two, drugs, sex – parts of addictive behaviours are deep wisdom at work to quieten a busy mind and allow space for processing and insight. Think that first slow deep drag on a fag (breath work) or deep mouthful of wine, simply letting a nervous system stop whirring. And some parts of addiction are running away, trying to block out what I believe about myself and others, a trauma response often easier to hide from than to look at and do the work on.

We have learnt to be frightened of discomfort and emotional pain looking at trauma, ego likes soft cushions and cashmere safety. Yet looking at it is where freedom lives. Trauma is a thought and chemical body response to an experience which I embody and gets wired into my system. It leaves an imprint that every time my mind sees something it thinks is similar, I feel and visit the whole experience again subconsciously, over and over; my mind gets caught up in the same old loop and prints it on everything. My body has a quieter memory until overload.

Be kind to yourself.

I COULD HAVE GOT A DIAGNOSIS

I sat in the bath every night for a year and cried. I was 28. I couldn't see a light at the end of the tunnel. I couldn't see a tunnel.

I went to the doctor and asked, "What's wrong with me?"

"Don't you come from a divorced family?" he said.

Something woke up. I never went back.

SOMETIMES

- I am angry at God.

- I am angry at absent fathers

- I am angry at Mum

- I am angry for all the kids and adults who hurt

- I am angry at all the healing I've had to do

- I am angry I spent so long NOT being them, that I wasted time not being me

And sometimes I astound myself in being unbreakable, so curious and brave.

FeraL

I avoid stuff to upset my equilibrium. To distant myself from wild emotions. To escape chaos, not be frenetic and mad. I lived emotional discomfort. I do not wish to touch that again, to feel the volcanic acid that means I disappear, void of a capacity to control anything but mostly myself. I cave in, crease inwards folding in concertinaed, crisp white lines of frantic, NOT THIS AGAIN. I thought I'd healed this panacea, a view so wide I'm engulfed in a world of constriction. Fighting for sanity, fighting for me. I died so many times inside. I want to be alive, simply alive to not touch the places that burned me down. It's not here now. I am not masochistic, it is self-preservation. What's wrong with choosing happy, welcome the bypass, hang the flags out, bake a celebration cake. The bypass is kind. I've never been kind. I've been raping myself for years never saying STOP, such a simple word.

Stop
STop
STOp
STOP

Don't light the old touchpaper please. I don't look back; back is feral and venom. Why would I hurt me again, would you tear yourself apart in the name of life when sanity no longer exists in the past? I hold it together here, here in my safety where I am alone, cossetted and loved in my own kindness and in remission to those who hurt with consistence. A uniform cut to fit the battle of pandemonium in which I snarled at the snags of frayed normality. I cried my soul in the torrential rain under the wind ravaged blue fir tree in my garden, the storm outside that raged and soaked me fragile outside half the cyclone of inside. An un-lucid mind, crippled by her words, her spitting, her bedlam. I would never be the victor – I didn't know how to be. I am simple in love, complex in hate, hurt and infliction. I vomit repression keeping a little bit back to shore me up, tuck me in at night to sleep well and be safe. I was buried and extinct in too little kindness, starved in a famine of loving. I never ever, ever, ever, ever, EVER want to be unhinged like an unclosed entrance to the lunatic that exists at the end of the touchpaper. I am the healing wounded soul hiding homogenised pasteurised and filtered. I don't shriek here like the lunatic lived.

I am a process.

I was not
created to find
my way home

but to know
that I am what
home is

Travelling Between Me

I don't know what to write.
I have an empty head.
No intellectual ideas.
How comfortable I am.
I am is a bag full of shit.
Spiritual people say I am.
Like, that's so simple.
I feel complex, messy and fucked up.
I am a fucked up, insecure, messy me,
Who is also the immensity of I am.
I am still learning to navigate
Both as one.
One is a minefield of ego,
The other is a completeness of no how-to-be.
On unstable ground as I cross from me to me.
I am both.
Only one.
Me.
I am.

I was created,
this georgia life,
I was chosen.
I matter.
I don't need to
know why

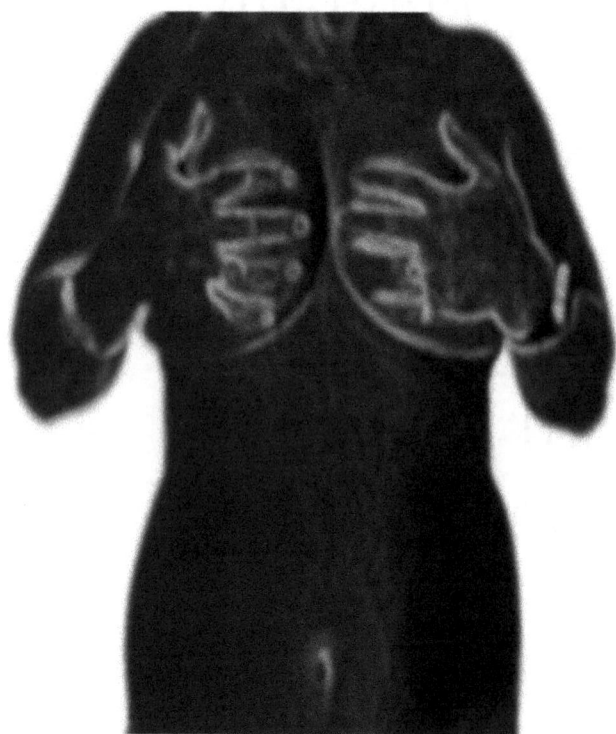

CHAPTER 6

BODY

PRIMAL INSTINCT

Seven days it took her to die   Seven days of tensioned
quiet   She stopped talking   Lay in self-chosen dying.

The nurse had duties.

Day five, I sat in Mum's room,
"That needs doing again properly," she said
As the nurse washed her vagina,
She turned to face me,
A face I don't know stared me down,
Animal.

I left the room,
Feeling like an interloper,
I witnessed primal.

Pleasure   Touch   Even in dying.

CHATTER

My body talks. This vessel that I don't control or programme. I didn't choose the shape, style, colour, size, heartbeats or cell division. My liver has healed itself; I don't know how. I had no say in this creation. I get different urges – hungry, tired or thirsty. My body is writing me love letters all the time, in a loop system of information of how the system is working. My body's always talking if I get quiet enough to listen. It will whisper quietly only for so long. Every experience leaves a note to be read at some time.

BEING MUM

Rag-bag of beautiful bones
Pain
Cut her down
No size
Little in harm
Hacked eyes
Tired
Of the round
About
About the hurt
About the shame
About the anger
About fuckery
Frazzled connection
Lean in
Closer
Have all that's mine
To give
Whilst you flicker.

GOING BACKWARDS

The pain in my chest stops me inhaling,
My hands slip on the china coffee cup,
Tacky armpits are stains on my T-shirt,
My belly is swollen volcanic,
A bladder that craves emptying hurts,
Weak legs that won't carry me any longer,
My stomach wants to projectile vomit,
A scream that's feral, escapes,
This body is battered.

I feel my imagination running wild,
Every nuance of this dis-ease,
A pulse of terror,
Over and over,
My body needs no reminder of
The past.
I sit in a chair at my desk
My head is not in this moment,
I'm exhausted.
She's fine, right now.

scam

We paint our pretty faces
With soda and lime,
To all look the same,
No freckles and blotches,
Chalk and wheat layer longer lashes,
Sodium and toxic for sweaty bits,
Some odd chemical concoction to aroma like the masses,
Metallic dye to change inherited skin,
A jab of poison to smooth out the lines,
Silicone pouty enhancement,
Bags in the boobs,
Gel in the buttocks,
Fluid fibreglass covers my calcium.
Plucked, ripped and lasered to be hairless,
My bonnet has everything on it
To be thicker, longer and luscious,
Blonde, auburn or peach,
A touch-up for roots.
Lipo for hips,
A labia fix,
Tuck the tummy,
Chisel the cheeks,
Remove the odd rib for an hourglass figure,
A pill to stop eating,
A tablet to cease absorbing,
A jab to look anorexic,
Peel off your skin,
Lift your eyes to look like a puss,

Pin in the ears,
Straighten your nose,
Replant hair to where it isn't.
Upsize a willy,
A hairline of stitches.
I am imperfect,
I am defective,
Plays to my insecure thoughts,
The marketing,
Such easy listening,
My happiness lives out here,
On the outside,
Bullshit,
Bullshit,
Bullshit,   BULLSHIT.
Happiness lives on the inside,
A state of mood,
Not from my mind,
But from where I look every morning,
The feel of my life,
The love in my heart,
No knife is necessary,
A change in my listening is all that's required,
Wellbeing is sown into my seams,
Where marketing doesn't exist.

Men-o-pause

I came late to solo orgasms. It was never a conversation
I had with my mother and the internet wasn't a thing. It
wasn't a sharing among the young women I knew. It's taken
ages to talk about it. I have a friend, Maxine, who says
even as a child it was always part of her life. Catholic friends
who don't. My body likes pleasure, I just thought it was for
two. I was married at 19. I had my first child at 25 after an
ectopic, second at 27 and third at 34. I lost a baby at 36
I didn't have time to grieve, lived with guilt and untouched
sorrow. Two years later went into perimenopause.

"I feel like something's being stolen and I don't have a
choice," I said. Philip and I lay in the bed I had inherited
from my father, the green taffeta folds and deep buttons
of the headboard faded on the right-hand edge where the
sun rested in the early morning light. The smell of a night's
sleep seeped from under the duvet and lay on our skin. My
blonde hair nested in troublesome sleep. My teeth, coated
from night toothpaste and the first sips of coffee, felt dirty.
The house was quiet with the kids still asleep, the stillness
before the morning storm of needs. I felt tight with the crime
of nature. My unused cervical cap sat on the bedside shelf
gathering dust.

"I want to choose when there are no more babies, how my
body changes," I said and cried.

I moved into 'after' fertile. My rhythm found its own self in different hormones and purpose. After a shower in an empty house sometimes my body feels horny, and it isn't about another. I am the source of my own pleasing whether it's solo or two, I need to be in the mood. The timing just happens.

perfection is just perception

THe Flavour

I wonder what it's like to make love to another woman,
To feel the soft swell of breasts mirroring mine,
Explore the vulva, the opening to birth,
Wet and coital, tender and open,
To be engulfed by another woman's tenderness,
Her laughter, her nurture, another mother of nature,
To be deeply bound in the energy of feminine,
Peacemakers, lovers, nourishers, birthers, creators,
Warriors and defenders,
The effervescent glow of divine womanhood,
There is a simplicity in sisterhood.
I've passed the competition for baby copulation,
The design to create a new being,
The rules of engagement become different,
A design of my body is non-essential or vaguely relevant,
It is deeper than that.
I've reached an age where labels seem pointless,
When it becomes about the soul you spend your life with,
The shape of my body, it seems to have been decided,
Should denote my sexual orientation,
The correct is the opposite sex,
Who made that up?
To love another of the same sex,
It's been historically decided, is something abnormal,
Mainly by the collar-wearing gender,
Something to hide behind heavy closed doors,
If a penis is what turns you on.
Cool.

It is about the energy of another human being,
Past my conditioning.
Life's about loving a being that's human.

we are
in this
world
but
not
of this
world

TIGHT-LIPPED

I fart, and then I apologise
Like I create wind.
I also burp and wee my pants sometimes.
I don't wear knickers
A habit I got out of during Covid
I wasn't going anywhere
No one to notice
I felt risqué to start with
Now they seem pointless
Another layer of public expectation
Unless I'm in a dress,
Lycra doesn't need them.
Things I'm told are socially unacceptable
Like bowel movements, or
Sex
I'm created to do it,
It's my gift too.
Why are some things to be kept hidden?
How can my biology be embarrassing
When we're all the same?
Sod tight-lipped beliefs
That make humanness dirty.

THE RUB OF GROWING SKIN

I live a biological process,
I am contained in skin,
It holds my contents together,
I am life in its form,
I'm very eco-friendly and have been recycled many times
Over,
It's personal to me this time,
I grow, and I shed,
It happens so painlessly and unnoticed by my body,
But my emotional journey of shed and growth is painful And
cathartic,
Stepping out of comfortable constructs about me has been
Like
Dry skin brushing with a cheese grater, and sometimes it
Hasn't,
I expand and contract, fuck it up or not, stretch or become
Rigid,
There is no one right way to live.
I arrived with a flavour,
I don't know what I came in with or why I am this flavour,
I did, and I am,
I'm pretty sure I've been here before as some other being,
I'm recycled life energy,
I'm guessing this is Georgia's first time, but I don't know,
Why I have my trials, tribulations, victories and Experiences,
I really don't know.
Seems to be my flavour is in the process of shed and
Growth,

My continued evolution,
My journey of birth, pathways and eventually biological
Death,
I don't understand why I hear thoughts that aren't helpful,
But I do,
Why the good ones are harder to believe,
It's how my brain is wired,
What I must overcome, my obstacles, my wins.
I am conscious living, creating, imagining, experiencing And
feeling,
Without it – living would be rather bland,
Like no salt, sugar or butter,
The rub of growing skin is simply living all my flavour fully,
In the journey of my revolution of recycled body and life
Energy.
Not too seriously.

SOMETIMES THE BUBBLE OF LIFE I AM THROUGH THE FOREST OF THOUGHT, IS NEARLY INVISIBLE.

WHaT IF?

My life is to play as a biological being,
An essence that enlivens this intelligent vessel.
If I misunderstand survival,
The simple reality of feeling thought,
It sends signals words get put to,
The container of millions of memories.
The body I didn't choose, is perfection,
It's the canvas of being a human.

Naked

CHAPTER 7

FINDING

2 For 1

I woke up on Wednesday night at 2.30 am, the bedroom was twilight with the light from my toothbrush on charge. The space I call my head a goldfish bowl — it contained my brain, with two Nikon lenses for eyes. On the inside surface I watched a film play from left to right, like the IMAX cinema at Waterloo Station. Outside the goldfish bowl were things, the velvet chair in the corner covered with clothes, the mahogany chest I got from my mother, my husband snored on. I lay there not wanting to breathe and to lose this clarity of how I walk through the world, seeing my own version of it. I watched a world of bodies all walking around in their own goldfish bowls, with their own unique films — it was surreal. I touched my cheek to check I was still here, and I wasn't asleep or delusional. I cried and kept mouthing holy fuck in silence. I heard I am the dream of the infinite dreamer, here to just dream whatever into being. I am dreaming only always, the finite dreamer. By 5 o'clock, my eyes sore, I needed to sleep. I was desperate not to lose this trip into truth without any substance abuse. I spoke about it live on the Insight Timer app on Friday and cried and babbled sometimes.

Today I can't see it, the truth, I'm back in my head. I drove to Guildford for Xmas shopping and screamed in the car, "What the fuck do you want from me?" to the infinite intelligence of creation, "Stop drip-feeding me! How can I flow in and out and remain in peace?"

Never broken
Nothing to fix

Sometimes it's just a bit
messy.

INNER CHILD

STAGE 1

I came complete,
I came without judgement,
I came as a learner,
I came as an explorer,
I came as a player,
I came as a creator,
I came as an inhabitant of a body,
I came free,
I came limitless,
I came as potential,
I came without seeing differences,
I came to love.

STAGE 2

I learnt I had to be clever,
I learnt I had limits,
I learnt I had to be better,
I learnt I had to compete,
I learnt to compete was the point,
I learnt there was winning and losing,
I learnt there was a norm,
I learnt I didn't fit the median,
I learnt happiness came from outside,
I learnt about myself from everyone outside,

I learnt everyone has the correct opinion,
I learnt to strive and set goals,
I learnt to not listen to my intuition,
I learnt to look outside of myself for the answer,
I learnt not to be just happy and present.

Stage 3

I am learning to unlearn the learnt,
I am deeper inner knowing,
I am limitless always,
I am complete and always was,
I am never broken and never was,
I am unlabelled,
I am pure creation,
I am always a beginner,
I am always the seed for my subsequent stage,
I am the ease of not knowing,
I am the comfort of freewheeling,
I am my inner child still as adult.

LIMITATION – WHERE ARE YOU?

I asked.
I heard.

"Be tender with me, I've come a long way, past broken
bridges and empty riverbeds dust-filled,
blown by vacant winds.
I've shattered contoured bones that were stuck and
snagged in a crevice of a blocked birth canal.
The small space that fitted well, as a child unparented in
calcium.
I am brittle. Ectopic I tightened as you grew.
My skin is faded by lack of sunlight
I moulded here washed by black.
Today you looked for me.
I've waited,
You offer me your hand.
Older than I remember it.
I got stuck and never grew up
The edges are sharp and gash as I leave hiding.
I am safe, you say
I hesitate to be in the light
To die to come alive."

FOUND

I found a child,
Lost in my body
Scared
She is me
Unknowing
Safety
I do the work
Write a new book
I wear adult shoes
Most of the time now.

serenely smug

At a party last night,
I was included,
It felt very nice
Warm and cosy inside my head,
Serenely smug,
Others came calling who were not invited,
Who got turned away.
I said calmly and piously in my head,
"It's life; we are all not included sometimes,"
Twenty minutes later, there were whisperings between
Frocks
About a concert on Sunday,
Who's at whose house,
Would they like to come?
Quiet mutterings in corners,
No invitation for me.
My poor me lifted her head pouting,
Full of indignation and 'pick me',
Ruffled my feathers for the rest of the evening.
Gone was my calm at not being included sometimes,
Piously offended kicked in,
I heard all the natter in my head,
It went on while I sipped my wine,
When I laughed and chatted,
It felt like acid,
I couldn't do anything with it, on it moaned
So, I left it alone, didn't feed it or show it any love,
It would get left out and wouldn't be included,

And eventually, quiet down.
It was a jazz concert,
I hate bloody jazz!
So please don't invite me,
Please leave me out.

SOME WOMEN I JUST LOVE

IF I GOT TO
CHOOSE AS THE
CREATOR WHAT
THOUGHT POPPED
IN, I WOULDN'T
HAVE ANY
THOUGHT I DIDN'T
LIKE...
HOW
IRONIC! ...

sauce

I say fuck a lot   I learnt that from my mother   I say
she taught me well after   She said Fucking idiot   or such
a lot   I kept fuck Fucking awesome   or fuck that   I
kept strawberry jam on a Sunday roast   Mayonnaise on
everything else.

ABSTINENCE

I sat in a woman's circle on a sunny Saturday afternoon in Glastonbury after a week of Ayahuasca. San Pedro was our last journey, working with two shamans, Maria and Sopa. I was eating a satsuma, it was sunshine orange and dribbled with juice, my mouth lined with sweetness. I was at one with it and nature, knowing my wholeness. I said, "These are fucking awesome."

Sopa looked at me from brown eyes of kindness and simply said, "Are you a bloke propping up some bar on a Saturday night talking about an act of aggression, or a sister in a holy sacred space filled with Love?"

I'm trying to abstain from using THAT word... I don't know how long it will last...

Liar

Life isn't fair,
I'm not being picked,
I'm not creating what I should be,
I'm coming last,
I'm getting old,
I'm eating too many carbs,
My arse is too big,
Why did two people I coached make decisions that Weren't in line with
What I thought they heard?
I'm judgemental; that isn't nice,
I want to be stripping and upholstering the chairs I Bought,
I wouldn't be creating what I should be,
I inherited my mother's pain,
I'm stuck in this,
I must be evolving quicker.

It started as a spark somewhere way deep and smouldered, so I fed it; it was hungry and ravenous; it had been foodless for a while because I knew it wasn't real when I knew it wasn't real; I knew the lies. The spark took hold of the bark of the first stick, engulfed, the spark became a flame. And one flame became two, and three and more until I had a campfire at which to sit around, the voices, the lies and me. We got very comfy and decided to make it bigger:

I am incapable,
Why can't I lose weight? Maybe it's emotional baggage,
(That's always a good one),
I shouldn't be thinking like this,
I know better,
I really do know better,
If I truly got this, I wouldn't be here.
I am a victim.

And the wind picked up and fanned the flames that danced a merry glow. Orange and red, russet and gold whisked up. My campfire, now an inferno, sucked and bled me dry. My chest got tighter, and my world got smaller. My merry dance, the overflowing of wellbeing, just left me high and dry.

I've gone back inside to see when the truth that I am whole became a lie. The pesky voices reside in my head; thinking to keep me safe, to be relevant always in the moments of my day. A streaming flow of lava burns on its way through, that I forget I'm born of peace that, like water, gently flows. I will rest in my inferno, knowing it isn't real, let the water flow from the source, and slowly come back to see that the voices in my head are not real; they are not me. I am the place where the well is full, overflowing and complete, the place I always know when I know it; that energy is me.

Passing Through

I feel it in my chest,
It's empty, so empty it's cavernous,
It's an empty stripped bare space.
I'm not used to feeling like this,
All my pent-up emotions,
No angst,
No suffering,
Is not here and it's frightening.
It's terrifying to not give a fuck,
The emptiness,
Where I can feel my heart pumping nervousness
In an empty open space that's ripe to
Experience something other,
Than painful wanting,
Wanting takes me away from peace.
I'd choose peace over wanting every day,
I'm just not used to it yet,
Peace seems kinder, alive and more spacious,
Than wanting ever did.

DO IT BECAUSE IT
SAYS NOTHING
ABOUT YOUR IMAGE
–

THAT'S MAGIC.

PAINTING BY NUMBERS - THE ART OF COUNTING

I want my kids to know they count to me.
Not because of what they do or do not.
Not because of how they dress or choose not.
Not because of who they are with or are not.
Not because of how they achieve or appear not.
Not because of anything they have or have not.
Not because of what they know or simply not.
Not because of anything other than their being.
They are perfect art.
They count to me.
I Love You.

Growing Skin

I look at the dust bunnies in the corner, and there is a mix of the pieces I've shed. Bits of daughter, mother, wife, lover and me. Some of the unhelpful bits that looked no longer true, and some simply escaped when I've been unearthing.

On the cream sofa is the overburdened daughter of expectation, pinned to the soft down pillow by the weight of my mother's outdated, frightened internal agenda. Wearing tweeds with pearl earrings, never quite comfortable in someone else's idea of sensible shoes but with room for a pony.

On the glass bookshelves filled with inspirational self-help books, are fingered footprints in a layer of me. Even thicker around the edges where the duster never dusted. All the searching paraphernalia to keep the glue together, to not naturally shed: to grow anew as I am designed to do. All the grubby turned corner pages to have to implement. All the books that told me I would be better if I only followed their wisdom because there was something wrong with me, they are bereft by abandonment. I seek my wisdom until it seems a conversation might be an answer.

Under the desk trapped in the white metal upright supports amongst the broken cobwebs, are my abandoned cells of the follower of wifedom — the freedom from compliance and duty set by the stereotypical society. I'm not reliant on marriage or any person for my sense of self identity. We travel together a beautiful journey, Philip and I. Happy cells are created by me and me alone. Society's cells hide in the corner.

Squatting under the grey mohair blanket is a dusting of me and my mother's and others of hand-me-down ideas about parenting, the boxes and corners to fit children in. Once I got over that, all I knew was to love them and set me and them free to live lives fully as wished. No agenda.

On the cable to the Mac, never noticed and never cleaned, is the haired globules remains of the needy friend, the needy woman, the needy me. I learnt the needy came from the believed lack in me. That I was weak without being propped up by others. Fear of being left out said I wasn't good enough. I wasn't in the boat with all others if the ship went down. I have my own boat now; I need no other vessel and am free to invite others into my boat or not.

Between the boxes of tarot cards and divination cards, next to the naked art canvas, are slithers of my hidden skin. I own my intuition now, the powers unseen. I adorn every page I write with channelled words from outside of my mind. I own my unique oddness; it's served me beautifully as the creative force of my being in this skin.

The lover who lurks in the drawer amongst the broken un-inked pens, disused keyboards and phone connectors, is flakes of my body. I'm in a quiet phase as I create something else.

The old ME is in the vacuum bag under the stairs with all the dog hair. ME was full of apprehension, victim, littledom, a big brassy presence with an empty silent voice, the perpetual searcher outside for my sense of balance, the messy one. With each peel, they get quieter, and they may never die, but the new skin I grow is me 2.0, whoever she is. She is brilliant.

A Forgotten Blessing

I love the smelly dogs on the
Bed, curled in the crook of my leg
With my morning cuppa.
I love that my windows always
Needed cleaning.
I had a child at home at
Twenty-six who asked
"What's for dinner?"
Who kissed me goodnight and
Said "I love you, Mum!"
I love I loved so many beings
I love that I wrote a book that
Wasn't planned and played with God's genius.
I love I berate myself
Tells me that
I am is alive.
I love that for some reason I
Got pissed off at the squirrels
Stealing the birds' nuts
That I have the capacity
To listen and sometimes not.
I get to love all kinds
Of stuff and hate some others
Not in equal measure,
I love that my recurrent UTIs
Are over,
The gift of a torn perineum three times over
Birthing — I'd do that again in heartbeat.

That maybe I impact someone's
Moment in a good way.
I love after the fact of my mother
I got to heal from that shit show
And love her just different.
I love I forget important stuff
Can say yes or no
Not knowing the right answer.
I love I got older
I love sucking a chocolate
Really slowly as it dissolves
On my tongue's pleasure.
I love bemoaning cellulite
I love my naked dimpled arse
On social media
That I shock some people.
I love a magic mushroom journey at 59,
Kissing the same man goodnight
For 40 years and sometimes wanting to leave.
I love I held an anorexic daughter tight
Bathed, fed her and watched her flourish,
That I fit under my son's chin for a hug.
I love I can fuck it up and also not
I could have just passed by and missed
The caressing of life in a blink of God's eye,
I love that I get to share a moment of my creation
I love I got a glimpse of truth
And that all I love
Will be forgotten.

NOTE TO SELF FROM DIVINE LIFE – SIMPLER BUT NOT SIMPLE

I keep trying to write something new, to tell you you're limitless.

Not the little boxed thing your mind tells you you are. I've written it hundreds of different ways, in all kinds of themes.

So here goes once more....................................
....
....
....

Your life is an intimately impersonal living.
You are not what you think.
You are having a human experience,
You are the feeler of it all.
You are not in control, but choices will be made,
You cannot choose a wrong path, it's just a path.
You are resilient.
You are your own healer.
You are perfect and whole.
You are created to create.
You are the greatest wisdom for yourself.
You are the universe in skin.
You are The Source.
You are the energy that is everything.
You are connected to everyone.
You are love.
You are life……..

· ·

It doesn't get any **bigger**.
And I can't say it simpler.

THE PARADOX

Sometimes, between being a slice of God and a human being, I get lost. The balancing of scales. Sometimes I think, sometimes I get lost in thinking still. I still fight it sometimes, the feeling of discomfort even though I know it's the illusion of a mind that acquired all sorts of ideas and it isn't me. I have picked so many scabs off beliefs in the angst of an uncomfortable feeling. I wouldn't say I love them and yet I do because I know something is bubbling to the surface to be seen. Something in my world is being reflected to me. It's often some sort of judgement I haven't seen the truth of yet. How to navigate a world which sometimes looks like such an illusion.

When I touch the depths of my soul, a place without any judgement and ideas, I come back to this lived human experience and it sometimes feels so tight. And then I remember how blessed I am that I got to say fuck, make love, write, fight, cry, laugh and eat and that's why I am here. In two generations, I won't be remembered; a copy of this book will be on the shelves of the British Library and maybe nowhere else. I will exist in the memory and energy of all things but be nowhere seen.

I am not frightened to die — I've seen and spoken with the other side. I suffer when I think how much I will miss but I don't think missing is a thing there. I'm reminded to slow down and be here now. I hold my own hand often as I go to sleep to remind myself there is part of me so loving and it never left.

My husband and my children are slices of God too and I have my glorious story of them. My mother often comes visit me now, she's different. I sat with my daughter the other day and felt my mother's absolute awe at this woman, the woman she really didn't see when she was here. It gives me such hope that we heal and learn we are love either in this life or the next. I feel that I totter between worlds, this is my paradox, the seen and unseen and being both. Forgiveness for confusion seems the way.

MOODS OF LOVE

Today I am love,
How very funny,
Because yesterday I was too,
But I was also in a bad mood,
And the day before, I was pissed off,
Didn't feel love at all.
Today I am bloated,
And my clothes will be annoyingly tight,
The week before, I was insecure,
About what I should be doing,
I wanted to know why I had
Not succeeded in ways I'd imagined,
Then I sat and wrote beautiful prose,
I was love in all of these.
I'll be love later when I plant my roses,
And when I cook dinner,
I may be in some sort of mood,
The mood is my human stuff,
Underneath I am love,
Something without muscle and moods,
Love, just watching all this happen.

EMBRACE BEING
NOBODY

LOVE BEING YOU

THe BIrTH OF WOrDS

The encoding of the all,
Umbilical cords of ribboned prose
Birthed into the world,
From stardust is created meaning,
All from hand-me-downs,
Pages of bodies living legged words,
Crocheted labia parcel forth virgin skin journals,
Baubles of life spat out by biodynamic propulsion,
Timed with expulsion,
Breathed by the infinite cosmos,
Lava sparks of illumination bound to boned spines,
Tick tock tick tock hours run away,
While time ripples like ice cream,
Cowboy worms carry love away,
Silver-legged spiders wrap the departed,
Blue lips cry for the lost,
The search for connection,
Flowing threads of postulation,
The nature of mother is a silken donor suit,
Her empirical core cooks dictionaries of wonder,
Speaking lollipops that drop into heaven
From soil we are born again,
Walking words.

TOTAL DISREGARD

I am the soul of a poet
I like to start early
Though sometimes I'm a night owl
With little regard for the Necessities of Life.
I astound myself in the appearance of words
Words that create something with a feel of cell Connection,
the fizz of freedom.
I am the home of endless creation
I'm so much bigger, fucking huge.
I don't do the jobs I'm meant to, I don't give a shit
I am creating a new world
Travelling time, space and matter.
I am the soul of a poet
Who doesn't care about
Dinner time or calories
I am greedy of human timing and beauty sleep
I am alive
The architect of my future one creation after the last.
I am the soul of a poet
A flavour with pinches of this and that mixed
I travel a single picture on a passport
The poet.

TrUST

I trust the sun will rise and descend.
I trust I will breathe till I die.
I trust there will always be something to write.
I trust something happens when it must.
I trust kings and queens will reign till they fall.
I trust I have my own reality, that everyone else's is different.
I trust cycles of abundance and famine.
I trust people will gossip and forget.
I trust babies will be born and the aged will depart.
I trust acorns to grow and leaves to fall when they must.
I trust the division and repair of cells when due.
I trust there will be plagues and miracles.
I trust in love and heartbreak to sing about.
I trust mankind will be here until they are not.
I trust there will always be laughter and tears.
I trust there will always be wars and kissing.
I trust below my suffering; I'm genuinely whole.
I trust life will be exactly as it is.
I trust it will all just go on as it will.
I trust I will forget to trust sometimes.
I trust whether I trust it or not is totally irrelevant.
I just like it that way.

Deeply Okay

My living is made of moments,
Merely moments,
Of it's not okay,
Covering over what is deeply always consistent,
That
I am
deeply okay,
I know this.

JUST a Happy Moment

James asked me
"Are you taking a selfie?"
"Yes," I answered.
"It reminds me that
Nothing causes me to be happy
Except me
Coz all I'm doing is
Sitting in the back seat
With nothing to do
But look out the window
And watch my journey unfold,
Listening to the natter
Of you two
And occasionally, like
A 5-year-old, lean on
The back of your seats
And smile at you both
From my heart.
I'm reminding myself
How my life is so simply
That,
Smiling from heart.
Smile for me,"
I asked
Snap
"A picture to remind me,
You do it too!"

SHE WAS ALWAYS
JUST LOVE
COVERED OVER.
SAME FOR ME TOO

THAT'S ALL THERE
EVER IS....

unearthing

I am being unearthed,
Moment by moment.
I'm finding the flavour of me,
What I like
What I don't,
What possibilities there might be,
No wrong or right,
Having not known this for most of my life.
Living in thoughts,
How outside causes how I feel,
Losing myself in the instability
Of I don't exist,
When I am not what I think I am,
None of us is.
The secret,
I live my visit to this humaning,
Knowing that I am spirit,
Exploring the edges of both,
The sheer vastness of what that is.
I live in the unknowingness
Of what comes next,
What I will trip over,
What will be revealed.
My living gives me insight to tell you about,
So, something might reveal itself,
Each time I create,
I unearth a little bit more,
Some more of me comes into the light.

The snake who doesn't shed will die,
Growing and shedding my layers,
I have no choice in the unfolding,
Though a choice in what direction I look,
It looks like,
That's truly beautiful to have no control,
It's where my freedom lives,
The unknowingness until the knowing arrives.

KNOWING – IT'S NOT rational BUT your BEING KNOWS.
THAT'S YOU, THE ESSENCE OF SOURCE SPEAKING
AND YOU'RE NOT LOSING YOUR MIND!

(YOU'RE HEARING THE GREATER MIND)

MY Fair Lady

The echo in my head of the only song I recall her with
The remembrance of something as a child of moments
shared
Notes from her youth
From her memories that made her smile
Maybe it was when I wouldn't sleep, and she remembered
Why sometimes she hadn't,
She sang just like Julie Andrews.
"I could have danced all night"…

I heal.

Somewhere she knew I was a dancer.

I PULSE

Wantonly caressed by the intimate throb,
Cells enlivened to seductive feral notes,
That pulse my sinuous body,
I am fully alive,
Bereft of groaning judgement,
I am lost unformed,
Living blissful connect to refined innate movement,
Adrift in the wild freedom of a biological body,
Craving a beat to vibrantly follow.
I am a delicious evoked being,
Let loose from caged mental confinement.
I am life effusively living
In the provocatively swaying hips
My rounded buttocks ached by forgotten pulsation,
Friction as silken inner thighs ignite each other
In the sweaty meeting of hot skin,
My eyes forgetfully focused internally, seeing beyond
That solid physicality the squats around me,
I am legs that instinctively know where and when
To meet the hard floor in the flow of the ecstatic moment,
Beads meander down my fluid spine to the
Hollow recess of my strapped back
Where my salty dress clings to the moisture.
Blonde tendrils of escaped hair float fearless in the air
Around my gyrating head, lithesome as water,
Destined to follow the whims of my fancy.
Lips synced to the faded memory of words,
Long unconsciously missed

That arise ghostly to be uttered with blind reverence
To the creative juice
That flowed them into a bland, unknowing mind,
That they were simply to be hooked, enthralled with each
other.
An ethereal invocation of the plethora of human emotion.
I dance.

safe

She was always trying to keep me safe as her understudy
Safe from the baby she had at 16   Safe from what
looked like danger to her   Safe from not doing it right
Safe from having to worry about money   Safe from ever
being in need   Safe from being alone   Safe from a messy
life   Safe from letting the side down   Safe with her in
control   Simply what safe meant to her

She loved me so she put me in her box to keep me safe
from her scabs and scars. She didn't know I'd have my own.

SHE DIDN'T SEE ME.
I UNDERSTAND NOW
SHE BELIEVED EVERY THOUGHT.
SHE HADN'T GOT A CLUE IT WAS ALL ABOUT HER
NOT ME.

SHOES OF FREEDOM

I have diamonds on the sole of my shoes now,
They are dead man's boots no longer,
I have boogie shoes and high heeled sneakers to dance in,
Blue suede shoes allow me to be footloose,
Walking in my shoes is no longer tight,
The angels want to wear my red shoes of cha-cha heels,
I am goody two shoes and dirty boots with nothing attached,
These boots were made for walking,
My heart's back in the right place,
The old brown shoes of my childhood have retired.

To all the songwriters above, I give thanks for all my
shoes…

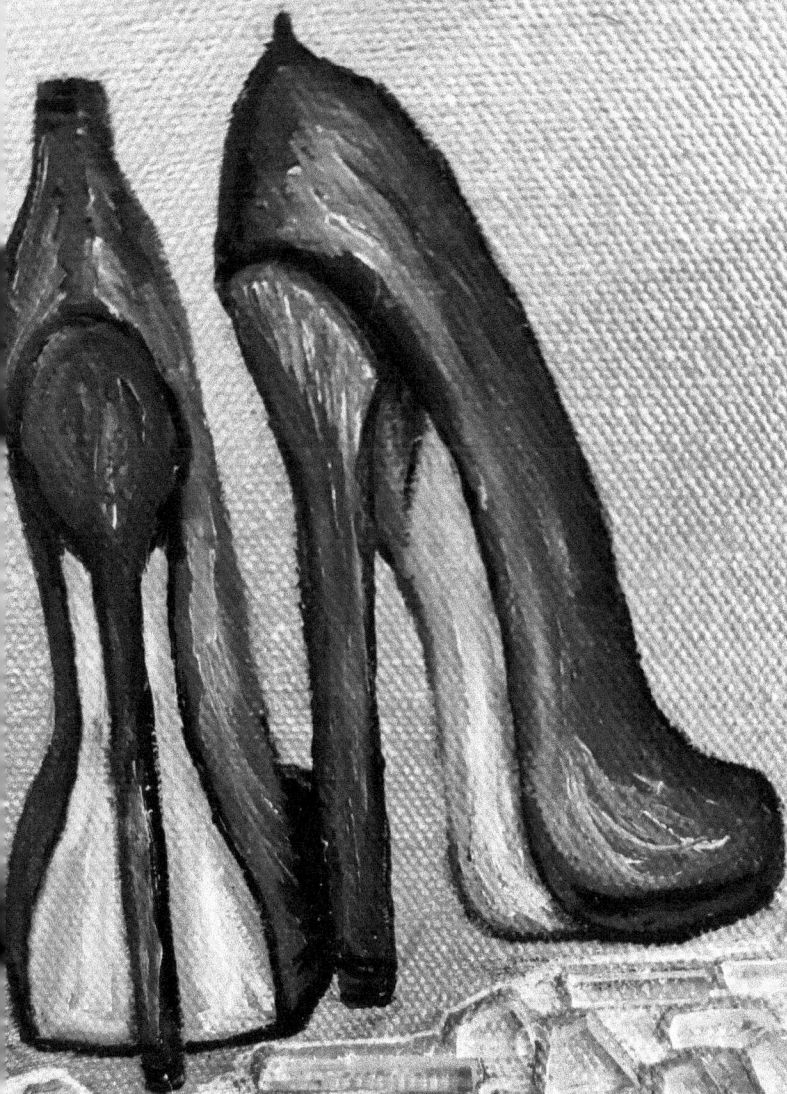

THE AFTER PARTY

I was lying in long grass, watching the clouds puff along in the sky, my anger spent, and my body tired from the release of bone grief, that my life here was not a punishment, a banning from heaven and the energy of oneness into the chaos of human separation, of being Georgia, the daughter of parents in pain who played out as narcissists.

No one ever told me I was a gift; they had told me plenty of other things which had become a version of beliefs about myself. I saw in the quietest of moments as the ears of grass blew across my view of the sky, that my life is the gift. I am a gift with many talents, knots and a beautifully creative mind. I get to feel it all and know I am shatterproof, truly and deeply, I am unbreakable at my very core.

I matter as matter, and the children of narcissism don't know this, I did not know this. Under our masks we never get a chance to see who we are. I was so busy in the last nine years of healing to be **Not Like Them**, that I still felt like a bud without the power to blossom. I've looked at what I don't want to be and what's scared me to be because that might be like my parents were. I forgot to bear witness to myself and forgot that there was no audience to play to except me.

I am consciousness woven into the fabric of a life named Georgia and she matters enough to have been created, to be here this time. I thank my parents as my biological creators, the ripples of them are part of the creation of me, how I am in the world, how I love. I am learning that I have to love myself as much as I love everyone else, I matter just as much. The more in touch with my flavour and fancies, the more I am in touch with theirs.

I saw my wholeness, unbrokenness and un-wrongness. Free of judgement, this meant I saw everyone's wholeness. Mind, Body, Spirit. Another step in reclaiming the gift of me and my life as pure creation in cells, bone and DNA.

In my wholeness I can stop picking at scabs, I can shed my old skin; a snake who doesn't shed will die in its old, constricted coat that it's time to let go of. This book was originally called *Growing Skin*, a title I'm still very fond of. I am life energy in a body suit of skin, a living organism, in one giant organism of life, unable with or without a body to be ever disconnected and the gift is I am here. I am energy, more space than matter, everything is. I fit in a thimble as biology.

I know who I am
I know what I am
I know how I serve
I am eternal
And my mother named me Georgia in this life.
I am.

And everything is abundance from there.

HOME

My freedom, My space,
Where the waves lap the land,
As they have always done,
How far they come is at the whim of the moon.
Memories get washed away in the tide,
Hearts and names drawn with sticks,
Disappear from the moment of joy,
When they came into being.
Shells, some barren,
Others full of life,
Hidden in the spirals unseen.
Toes dipped in chilly sparkles,
Sandy turn-ups on jeans,
Pockets jangle with pebbles and shells,
That fill car doors on leaving.
Children run chased by stampeding froth,
Eyes brightly alive in the race,
Tsunamis of sand carry bottoms laughing through dunes,
Footprint puddles of those once here.
Shipwrecks of flotsam and jetsam,
Some plastic bags slippery with bacteria,
An odd child's shoe from who knows where,
A child a mother told off for being careless.
My salty lips cracked,
Licked by a pink tongue,
Matted hair stuck to an abrasive neck.
Dogs not allowed until after September,
Hands held in loving links of meanderings,

Seagulls swoop through thermals,
Squawking disturbed by humans,
Stealing from crisp packets, abandoned.
I've danced on this beach at sunrise,
AirPods thumping rhythm, my body mastered,
As the joggers' determined thighs fight the sand,
Passed me by, a quizzical look at my madness.
Long golden shadows as the sun settles,
Ablaze in the watered crimson horizon,
The end of another seaside day,
Hot chocolate and marshmallows,
Silences windy induced hunger.
This is my place, that I share with others,
Where the seas of my soul,
Meet the land of my humanity.

NORMAL
PEOPLE
SCARE
ME

DON'T TAKE IT
PERSONALLY

HEALING IS
UNDERSTANDING

FORGIVENESS IS
BEING DONE

THE SECOND QUESTION...

"WHAT WOULD LOVE DO?"

LISTEN....................

WHILE YOU PUT YOUR OWN OXYGEN MASK ON....
THAT'S YOUR ONLY JOB, "YOU."

DON'T WISH FOR MORE

This is it,
The all,
The everything of Life,
Every breath, tear or giggle
Nothing is lacked
I don't wish for more
Everything is present
In life already.
Is this all there is?
Yes, and it's fucking brilliant
It's just I forget this
I forget life is a miracle
And I am its gift.
When I think it's all about
The irrelevant
As I gaze at the world
From possibility I am amazed
Is this all there is?
Yes, and it's bloody brilliant
I don't wish for more
A waste of valuable time
It's all the miracle
I got the lottery win
I could have just passed by

I dip, taste and savour it
This is all there is
I don't wish for more
I am the gift of a miracle in plain sight.
I am creation.

AHO MITAKUYE OYASIN -

we are all related

THE TOOL

Everything is just one thing. We are an evolution of conscious energy come into a 3D experience.

Thought is energy that flows through a mind that is translated into words. Two different things that work together to give an experience of life and communication — imagine if I couldn't talk. ☺ A tool this body uses in life. Not what we are. My thoughts are yours and yours are mine, a universal medium misunderstood. Words and feelings become our healers and experience when understood, they give texture, creative juice and a lived experience — use your words wisely, lovingly and powerfully to create your world. There is only this time around until there's another energy cycle.

9/8/2025 - THE SHARD THAT SLICED

A cornflower blue sky my blanket
I lay on the wooden altar
Grey sheepskin soft under my bones
She played the drum of stretched cow hide
With clubs in a slow deep rhythm
A beat of indigenous Navajo
I felt him stand next to me
Not seen to the eye
He hushed me as he reached into my heart
Found the floating chip that broke off
9 years ago as I watched my mother die
In her toxic destructive way
That tried to destroy me
He crumbled it between two fingers
Dust blown away by a kind wind
The final piece of healing.

MY TRUTH

I understand.

I forgive.

I loved my mum, still do, the silly cow.

Georgia Bazin

Deepest Thanks:
To Writing.

Three years ago, when writing was the next nudge, I was delivered a writing teacher called Jules Swales (Julesswales. com). She teaches the "Jack Grapes' Method Writing."

I gave up a Friday night social life to attend class, 5pm to 7.30pm – in three years I've missed three classes. Doesn't matter where I am in the world – I attend, sometimes in a bikini on a beach, possibly to the chagrin of fellow Zoom attendees.

Jules will always say this is not therapy. No, it is something deeper, I call it God coaching god. It has allowed the deepest parts of my psyche, humanity and spirit to become visible and then the allowance of love and truth to come through, for new truths to be known and something new to happen, a change in narrative, a new truer novel of me.

We forget all great books have many edits, often whole rewrites, yet forget to do that about ourselves. We are a canvas – a novel of words, words are the tool in which we appear. Choose them wisely and don't forget the fucking eraser!

ADDITIONAL THANKS TO:

Gratitude and love to Sara Priestly of Inky Paw Books (www. thoughtfulraven.co.uk) for her immense patience and creative eye for finetuning my book cover.

Zara Thatcher — www.printreadyeditorial.com
Such patience, calmness and professionalism.

Also

Olivia Eisinger — oliviaeisinger@icloud.com
Editor and the first person to ever say to me, "Please don't ever listen to anyone who ever says you can't write."

A timely reminder and clarity for My head. ☺ I am a writer, and I thank you, Olivia. Much Love.

References:

Foreword:
Alice Miller, *The Drama of the Gifted Child: The Search for the True Self,* (Das Drama des begabten Kindes, Original German edition, Suhrkamp 1979) Basic Books, 1979

Naked:
https://www.hubermanlab.com/episode/rick-rubin-protocols-to-access-creative-energy-and-process

Waking With Angels:
Sydney Banks quote

Peter the Repeater:
Daily Mail article – Monday 10th March, 1986

"It's Time" I heard:
Michael Neill, *The Inside-Out Revolution*, Hay House, 2013

My Fair Lady:
My Fair Lady, musical by Alan Jay Lerner and Frederick Loewe, 1956.

Shoes of Freedom:
Paul Simon – *Diamonds on the Soles of her Shoes*
Sting – *Dead Man's Boots*
KC & the Sunshine Band – *Boogie Shoes*
Tommy Tucker – *High-heeled Sneakers*
Elvis – *Blue Suede Shoes*

Kenny Logins – *Footloose*
Depeche Mode – *Walking in my Shoes*
Elvis Costello – *The Angels Want to Wear my Red Shoes*
Eartha Kitt/Bronski Beat – *Cha-cha Heels*
Adam Ant – *Goody Two-shoes*
Sonic Youth – *Dirty Boots*
Nancy Sinatra – *These Boots Were Made for Waling*
Elton John – *My Heart's in the Right Place*
The Beatles – *Old Brown Shoe*

INDEX

FOREWORD 1

DAUGHTER TO MOTHER 5

PROLOGUE 7
    NAKED 7
    WALKING WITH ANGELS 9
    LADLE WITH LOVE 11
    SKINNY DIP 16

INTRODUCTION 19
    BEGINNING 19
    CHIMERAS 23
    FUCK OFF 25

OVER DRESSED 27

CHAPTER 1 - THE CREATION 29
    WOMB 31
    CANVAS 32
    ITS SURVIVAL 34
    ONE WORD EMBROIDERED AT A TIME 37
    ABSENCE 39
    SECRETS ARE CARNAGE 42
    UGLY 44
    BIOLOGICAL 45
    PETER THE REPEATER 47

BARE FEET 50
JAMES 51
MY BLACK EYE 53
DANCE LIKE NO ONE IS WATCHING 56

CHAPTER TWO - THE HURT 59
MIRRORS 60
BELIEVER 63
SELF-HARMING 64
I AM STUPID 66
COME SIT WITH ME 67
GREED 69
BROKE 70
I'M FINE 71
SLASHER 72
DROWNING IN POISON 73
LOOKING FOR LOVE 75
LOOKING FOR SAFETY 76
UN-LABELLING 79
ONE YEAR LATER 80

CHAPTER 3 - MESSY STUFF LIVING 85
LEADER TABLE 87
I BLEW UP AN ALFA-ROMEO 88
SHIT AND THE FAN 91
THE FUCK GROOVE 92
THE SOUL OF AVOIDANCE 95
LABELS 97
EVERYONE NEEDS 99
CLUTTER OF WORRY 101
WHICH THERAPY TODAY? I'M SICK 102

ADVICE   103
THE WRONG MATHS   104
TAILORING   107
SOMETIMES IT JUST DOESNT WORK   109

CHAPTER 4 - THE UNSEEN   113
   THE VEIL   114
   UNAGREED HAUNTING   115
   HOW I AM WIRED   116
   HUMAN HURTS   117
   CONVERSATIONING WITH THE DEAD   121
   DEARLY DEPARTED   123
   A VISITOR I DONT MIND THESE DAYS   124
   PLATFORM PSYCHIC   125
   SEEN IT ALREADY   128
   PATIENCE   129
   MUM WAS A WITCH TOO   130

                UNDRESSING   131

CHAPTER 5 - LOSS   133
   "ITS TIME", I HEARD   137
   I QUESTIONED   139
   SORRY IS SIMPLE   141
   SHE CALLED   142
   GENIUS CATALYST   143
   DONT DO FAINT-HEARTED   144
   PRAYING (ODE TO MICHAEL NEILL)   146
   HFMOG   150
   TRUTH   151

I DISAPPEARED IN THE SHOWER   154
HEALING THE CHILD   157
ROLODEX   161
WHOEVER SAID THIS AWAKENING STUFF'S EASY, WAS LYING 162
I SEE YOU UGLY   165
THE BURIAL   167
HI, I'M EGO   168
ADDICTION AND ANXIETY   171
I COULD HAVE GOT A DIAGNOSIS   172
SOMETIMES   173
FERAL   174
TRAVELLING BETWEEN ME   177

CHAPTER 6 - BODY   181
PRIMAL INSTINCT   182
CHATTER   183
BEING MUM   184
GOING BACKWARDS   186
SCAM   187
MEN-O-PAUSE   190
THE FLAVOUR   193
TIGHT-LIPPED   197
THE RUB OF GROWING SKIN   198
WHAT IF?   201

NAKED   203

CHAPTER 7 - FINDING   205
2 FOR 1   206
INNER CHILD   208

LIMITATION - WHERE ARE YOU?   210
FOUND   211
SERENELY SMUG   213
SAUCE   217
ABSTINENCE   218
LIAR   220
PASSING THROUGH   222
PAINTING BY NUMBERS - THE ART OF COUNTING   224
GROWING SKIN   226
A FORGOTTEN BLESSING   230
NOTE TO SELF FROM DIVINE LIFE -
SIMPLER BUT NOT SIMPLE   233
THE PARADOX   236
MOODS OF LOVE   238
THE BIRTH OF WORDS   241
TOTAL DISREGARD   242
TRUST   243
DEEPLY OKAY   244
JUST A HAPPY MOMENT   246
UNEARTHING   249
MY FAIR LADY   252
I PULSE   253
SAFE   255
SHOES OF FREEDOM   256
THE AFTER PARTY   258
HOME   260
DONT WISH FOR MORE   266
WE ARE ALL RELATED   269
THE TOOL   270
9/8/2025 - THE SHARD THAT SLICED   271
MY TRUTH   272

BE WHAT DESIRE FILLS YOU
WITH ALIVE EXCITEMENT,
FOCUS THERE
WATCH FOR THE MIRACLES
DO NOT FORGET
YOU ARE THE BIGGEST
MIRACLE OF ALL

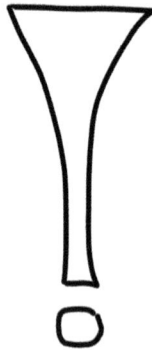

!

CREATED BY LOVE FOR LOVE.

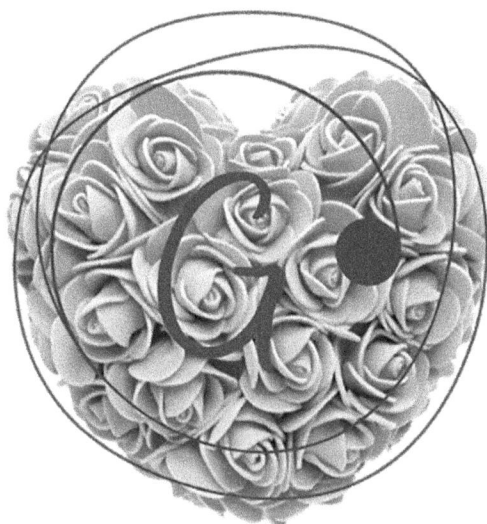

GEORGIA BAZIN

THE NAKED TRUTH - LOVE IS ALL THERE IS